DESTINATION
SAN FRANCISCO

Golden Gate Bridge, the most beautiful suspension bridge in the world.

DESTINATION
SAN FRANCISCO

Photographs: Axel Schenck
Text: Wolfgang J. Fuchs
Karl Teuschl

WINDSOR BOOKS
INTERNATIONAL

A row of colourful Victorian houses in Broderick Street bear witness to the joie de vivre so typical of San Francisco.

CONTENTS

Downtown San Francisco from Twin Peaks, with Market Street in the centre of the photograph.

THE DREAM CITY

It was pop star Scott McKenzie who told the world in 1967: "If you're going to San Francisco, be sure to wear some flowers in your hair." He was merely indicating in melodic form the degree of popularity this California dream city enjoyed at the time, particularly among young people. It is quite easy to find oneself using a fashionable cliché like "dream city", which is perhaps why many cities today are described in this way even though, in reality, they are more of a nightmare for the people living in them or visiting them. Leaving aside, however, the little problems of everyday life, which can become tedious anywhere in the world, there are still some places left which are well worth dreaming about. San Francisco is such a place.

The port of San Francisco is both the starting point for people wanting to see the world and the goal of many such people. It is a town where many different cultures converge and a market-place for both goods and opinions. Built like Rome on hills, San Francisco also certainly qualifies as a picture-book city. In spite of its relatively short history, the city has been marked by decisive historical events to such an extent that it can truly be said to have a life and character all of its own. The influences which have been brought to bear on San Francisco as a result of its trade with the Far East have nevertheless not prevented it from being considered one of the most European cities in America, whereas in the eyes of the world it ranks at the same time with New York and Los Angeles as being a typical American city. This means that San Francisco is, on the one hand, part of the American myth; on the other hand, however, it has become a myth in its own right, with its mixture of attractive city planning, cosmopolitan atmosphere and history.

San Francisco owes its legendary reputation not least to its many opposites, its wealth of contrasts. Situated on a peninsula and facing another peninsula to the north is the Bay of San Francisco, probably the largest natural harbour in the world. Owing to its many hills, however, San Francisco seems less like a coastal town and more like an inland settlement. Sea and mountains. The proximity to the sea and yet a sense of distance from it are united here in a most unusual way. In spite of the hills on which San Fran-

cisco was built the city was planned on a rectangular basis. The contrast also means that the city is one of the most eye-appealing places in the world, not least because of its typical Victorian wooden houses and quake-proof skyscrapers. And in spite of all the city planners' straight lines, the city still manages to catch the imagination.

There will scarcely be anyone who hasn't seen pictures of San Francisco at some time or other, for it is present everywhere on screens and billboards, the picturesque setting for drama and romance. San Francisco is a centre of the arts and joie de vivre, a vital, modern city with a great deal more tradition and history than would seem to be the case at first sight.

The Beginnings

Long before the white man set foot on the peninsula of San Francisco the Indians knew and treasured the location because of the salt that could be won from the marshy land, with all the dangers involved because of the tides. The mountain mint, which grows here to abundance, also made the area very attractive.

But all this was unknown to the first seafarers from Europe who sailed along the California coast in the sixteenth century: Fortune Ximes came in 1534, Joan Rodrigues Cabrillo in 1542, and on 17 June 1579, Sir Francis Drake dropped anchor a few miles northwest of San Francisco Bay. He laid claim to the land in the name of his Queen, Elizabeth I, and called it New Albion. As we all know, New England developed on the east coast of America as a colony of England, whereas the west coast later fell into Spanish hands.

The Spaniards had been looking for a harbour in the region for a long time, to serve as a base for the trading vessels in the Pacific and to make the journey to Manila and the Far East easier. They really only began to search in earnest when Catherine II became czarina and they were faced with the possible threat of Russia laying claim to the Spanish colonies from California down through Mexico and as far as Peru. Seven years after Catherine ascended the throne, the Spaniards discovered the area around San

Old St. Mary's Church, built in 1854, stands on the edge of Chinatown at the corner of Grant Avenue and California Street, down which the cable cars of the Embarcadero / Van Ness service rattle.

Francisco. The Spanish expedition which was the first to take a closer look at the bay, in October 1769, had not, however, discovered it from the sea but had approached over land. Like so many other great discoveries, this one was also the result of coincidence.

After this, the Spaniards reappeared in the area again and again. In 1772, for example, Pedro Fages and Pater Crespi camped on what is today the site of the University of California; the "San Carlos" under the command of Captain Juan Manuel de Ayala was at anchor in the bay from 5 August until 8 September 1775. The first Spanish colonists settled in the bay the following year. They named their village "Yerba Buena", good herb, after the mountain mint which the Indians before them had already prized.

(Some two hundred years later it was a completely different plant which was to attract pop and sub-cultures to the area, so from this point of view the name of that first settlement was well chosen.)

The settlers of 1776 were accompanied by Spanish monks and soldiers. Padre Junipero Serra, the man said to have founded the twenty-one Spanish missions along the Camino Real, also encouraged the building of "San Francisco de Asìs", which was consecrated to Saint Francis of Assisi on 17 September 1776. That same day the Spanish lieutenant José Joaquin Morega moved into his official residence, the "Presidio", a hut surrounded by a fence of palisades. Whereas the bay retained the name of the Italian saint, the mission was later given a new name. The early discoverers had called the bay "Laguna de Nuestra Señora de los Dolores" and in memory of this, the mission of San Francisco de Asìs became the Mission Dolores. It is still one of the special sights in San Francisco, and receives thousands of visitors every year.

The founding of Yerba Buena and the building of the mission and the Presidio marked the beginning of forty-five years of relative peace under Spanish rule. It was, by the way, the last time that Spanish colonizers struck out northwards from Mexico, as the power of the Spanish rule in the world was noticeably decreasing. Russia, France, England and the newly-developing United States of America all coveted this region on the Pacific coast. For the time being, California became a Mexican territory.

After Mexico became independent of Spain on 27 September 1821, it laid claim to California as part of the new republic. While it was a Mexican province, California was a sparsely-populated area devoted mainly to raising cattle. The young republic of Mexico proved, however, to be a much weaker ruler than the Spanish had been. The Mexican governors were replaced frequently and under their much laxer rule, Yerba Buena became a market-place for Russian and American goods. Smuggling became a profitable business in the face of which the Mexican authorities were virtually powerless.

The sound of a powerful Harley Davidson engine is an intrinsic part of the California way of life. This is Grant Avenue, the main thoroughfare in Chinatown, with the typical street signs in two languages (top left).

San Francisco's financial district, with its skyscrapers and glittering façades, begins where Montgomery and Post Streets join Market Street. The monument here commemorates California's joining the Union as the 31st state in 1850.

10

Union Square is the centre of metropolitan life in San Francisco with its elegant department stores, hotels, theatres and major airline offices. The Market Street to Aquatic Park/Fisherman's Wharf cable car runs down the west side of the square. The victory column is in memory of the Spanish-American War of 1898.

Even when the sun is at its strongest it is never oppressively hot in San Francisco as there is always a fresh breeze off the Pacific blowing through the city on the bay. This balloon-seller at Fisherman's Wharf has to maintain a tight hold on his balloons to keep them from blowing away.

Americans merchants, first and foremost among them the Hudson's Bay Company, demonstrated an ever-increasing interest in Yerba Buena and the Bay of San Francisco. Andrew Jackson, the seventh president of the United States, offered the Mexican government 500,000 dollars for the bay and the land around it. Mexico, however, gave the United States to understand that it had absolutely no intention of selling California.

The idea of creating a union which stretched from the east to the west coast of the continent was one which was dear to the American heart. The annexation of California was the goal everyone was working for, under the name of manifest destiny, obviously a decision of fate. James Knox Polk, the Governor of Tennessee, also supported the expanionists. He was elected eleventh president of the United States in 1844 and owed his electoral victory largely to his promise that he would bring California into the American confederation of states.

The Gold Rush

President Polk kept his promise. The ostensible reason for the war against Mexico which began in 1846 was the settling of the boundaries of Texas, also still part of Mexico. But the war in Texas spread to California, as this territory also had to be protected against British claims. In June 1846 there was a rebellion in California among the American settlers and ranchers who had gradually acquired large areas of the formerly widespread lands belonging to the missions. The aim of their rebellion, known as Bear Flag Rebellion, was simply to rid themselves of Mexican rule. The American captain Montgomery sailed into Yerba Buena in his ship "Portsmouth" on 9 July 1846 to support the American claim. The Mexicans offered no resistance and by eight o'clock in the morning of the same day the American flag was flying over the Presidio. After this event life continued much the same as ever for the somewhat more than four hundred people living in the village.

Somehow or other, however, the changes that had taken place had to be registered: the name of the village was changed to San Francisco on 30 January 1847. It grew slowly and would have remained a provincial outpost for some time if it hadn't been for Johann August Sutter, who lived one hundred-forty kilometres (eighty-seven miles) away on the American River and who had first set foot on California soil near the San Francisco Bay in 1839.

Sutter owned a sawmill and one of his carpenters, Wilson James Marshall, discovered several grains of a yellow metal on the land belonging to the mill on 28 January 1848. Gold! Sutter did everything in his power to stop the

discovery from becoming public knowledge, as he was concerned about his property and afraid he would not be allowed to continue with his agricultural experiments. But the discovery could not be kept secret and the news that enormous amounts of gold had been found in the legend-ary "El Dorado" of California spread like wild-fire through-out the region and abroad. The gold fever spread and thousands set out to make their fortunes and San Fran-cisco was, of course, the port in which these gold-diggers from overseas arrived. American prospectors also came to San Francisco, either to buy equipment or to treat them-selves to all kinds of luxuries with the gold they had found. They swarmed out from San Francisco, burrowing their way even as far as the Sierra Nevada mountains in their search for the precious metal.

There were, however, also other "gold-seekers" who came to San Francisco: men and women who wanted to make money quickly and people who realized that trade would become very lucrative in the California com-munities as a result of the gold rush. The population of California jumped to 25,000 within two years.

As Sutter had foreseen, crime also came with the gold: between December 1849 and June 1851 San Francisco was almost burned to the ground in six outbreaks of fire. Five of these were the result of arson, in all probability in order to cover up other crimes, mainly looting. The worst of these series of robberies was the responsibility of a group of discharged soldiers who had ganged together at the end of the war with Mexico in 1848, committing a number of crimes under the name the "Hounds".

The "People's Court" of newspaper publisher Sam Brannan put an end to their activities in July 1849, but then the "Sydney Ducks" took over and continued to terrorize the streets of San Francisco. Most of the latter were pris-oners allowed out on parole who had made their way to America from Sydney in Australia. In 1851 the first vigilante committee was formed in an attempt to put an end to their unscrupulous activities.

This militia was indeed successful in its attempt to ease the tension of the situation. It also soon became clear that there were honest people, too, who had come to Califor-nia in pursuit of happiness. One of these was, for example, Levi Strauss, who had emigrated to San Francisco from Bavaria in 1850. Of all the goods he had brought with him from the good old country all he had left after several un-successful business deals were bales of canvas for making sails. As the material was of no use to the prospectors for making tents, Strauss hit upon the idea of making it into hard-wearing trousers for the men and before he knew it he had found success. His idea gradually developed into

an industry: the trousers were popular because they did not tear and Strauss' "blue jeans" were soon drawing crowds of buyers, for the time being, however, only on the American market. A hundred years later these virtually indestructable trousers were carrying Levi Strauss' name and the name of his new home, San Francisco, all over the world. They have also had an admittedly decisive effect on the youth culture and fashions of today.

By the time Strauss arrived in San Francisco there was only one detail lacking in order to make California completely American: entry into the union of the United States of America, under whose protection the people of California had been since the end of the war against Mexico. This was achieved on 9 September 1850, when California became the thirty-first state in the Union.

Belonging to the United States did not at first prevent San Francisco from attracting less than honest people. In 1856 the vigilantes again cleared the town of gamblers and corrupt politicians. After this gambling, prostitution and gangsters tended to centre on the infamous "Barbary Coast", which retained its dubious reputation right up to the beginning of World War I. Chinatown also had a bad reputation for a time, but this was largely due to the fact that the Americans did not always fully understand certain aspects of the Far Eastern culture which had been imported by the Chinese, and partly also due to malicious campaigns by unscrupulous politicians.

Culture

The wealth and plenty which San Francisco had enjoyed since the gold rush did not, however, only serve to highlight the less attractive aspects of human nature. They also provided the foundation for the development of a way of life in California's great city which included the arts and culture. The architecture of the many restaurants, hotels and theatres, four of which were opera houses, was sumptuous. When the Italian opera star Tetrazzini came to perform in San Francisco, her coach was pulled along Market Street by her fans and she sang one of her arias for the people in the open-air, to the reward of frenetic applause from the excited crowd.

During the Civil War (1861–1865) and in the years immediately afterwards, San Francisco developed into one of the country's literary centres. It was here that Bret Harte founded his literary circle and played a considerable role in decentralizing American literature, increasing the importance of regional literature. In the course of his work for the magazine "Overland Monthly", he had noticed that it never contained stories about California or the other western territories. So he wrote one himself and thus created a new genre, the short story based on a regional topic with a journalistic influence.

There is still a hint of more modest standards in the hypermodern financial district at the north end of Market Street, where the classical skyscrapers of the turn of the century have no difficulty making a stand among the glass-fronted tower buildings of our day. The cable cars turn at the bottom of California Street (bottom right in the photo).

San Francisco is laid out like a giant chessboard. To the north and east a view can be had of the Bay, here down Spear Street south of Market, with the eastern end of the Bay Bridge.

14

Experts consider it to be a successful example of modern city architecture: the Embarcadero Center at the northern end of Market Street. The site also houses the Hyatt Regency Hotel with its unusual hall, almost one hundred metres (328 feet) long and sixty metres (197 feet) wide. The interior is aesthetically cool and impressive with its glass elevators and Charles Perry's sculpture "Eclipse".

Samuel Longhorne Clemens, who had been closely involved in the stormy development of the American West, prospecting for gold in Nevada for example, used to write humorous anecdotes for his brother's newspaper before moving to San Francisco in 1864 and changing his name to Mark Twain. He got a job as a reporter on the "Daily Morning Call" and joined Bret Harte's circle, the first step on his path to world-wide literary fame.

In one of the stories Mark Twain wrote about his time as a gold-miner and about San Francisco, he used the name "Frisco" on one occasion. This shortened version of the name developed around 1869, if the lexicographers are to be believed, and occurs again and again in the works of

other authors, some of them natives of the town. And yet it must be mentioned here that the residents of San Francisco considered the shortened form of Frisco to be rather more of an insult than a nickname.

The development of America's transport system also contributed extensively to the spread of literature. The most important milestone was the completion of the first transcontinental railroad from New York to San Francisco on 10 May 1869. Wells Fargo, the California transport company founded in 1852, had been far-sighted enough to get involved in the development of the railroad and was thus able to survive the era of the stage-coach.

Jack London, the writer, can be said to be an exclusive product of San Francisco. He was born in Oakland on the other side of the bay and later became a member of a youth gang known as the "Oyster Pirates" in San Francisco. After many adventures at sea and on land, he settled down and set to work on improving his social status, spending hours on improving his education. He used his experiences in Alaska as material for his first volume of short stories, which was published in 1900. His most famous book, "The Call of the Wild", was written in 1903. Together with "Sea Wolf" and "Martin Eden" it ranks among the classics in world literature and has frequently been made into films and used for television.

A Setback and A New Beginning

San Francisco was well on the way to becoming a peaceful, middle-class town which made no secret of its wild past, indeed was even mildly proud of it, still is today. The city had, after all, developed at a tremendous rate and its citizens had tried to get the best out of the situation. A great deal had been done to promote art and literature and, in spite of the speed at which the town had developed, the city fathers had shown considerable foresight on several occasions. For example, a law was passed in 1870 which reserved an area of about four square kilometres (one and a half square miles) on the western side of town for Golden Gate Park, today one of San Francisco's major attractions.

On the morning of 18 April 1906, however, all seemed to have been in vain. The worst earthquake in the history of California shook the town to its very foundations, destroying about eighty percent of the buildings. As, however, relatively few people actually lost their lives, the will to rebuild the town was strong.

Only someone who has heard the eerie rumblings of an earthquake and experienced the feeling of helplessness which prevails when the house around one suddenly starts to creak and shake can possible guage the degree of courage, or ignorance, involved in re-building the town on a site that is beautiful but greatly endangered. And indeed, reconstruction was not undertaken in an irresponsible way. It was not simply a matter of wanting to retain the attractive location of the city, the residents also wanted to be able to live peacefully and so greater attention was paid to making the new buildings quake-proof. Particularly in the case of the skyscrapers in the city's central Financial District, all possible precautions to make the buildings resistant to periodic tremors were taken.

Five years after the great earthquake San Francisco had risen again, like a phoenix from the ashes, to new glory on the same old hills. To celebrate this new beginning the town mounted an exhibition in 1915, the Panama Pacific World Exhibition, completely in the tradition of the great

The fashions in the many boutiques in San Francisco are as unconventional and easy-going as the California way of life. While fewer designer fashions may be found, you will find, instead, a wealth of casual, comfortable clothes with an individual touch, such as here in a shop on Stockton Street.

Continued on page 22

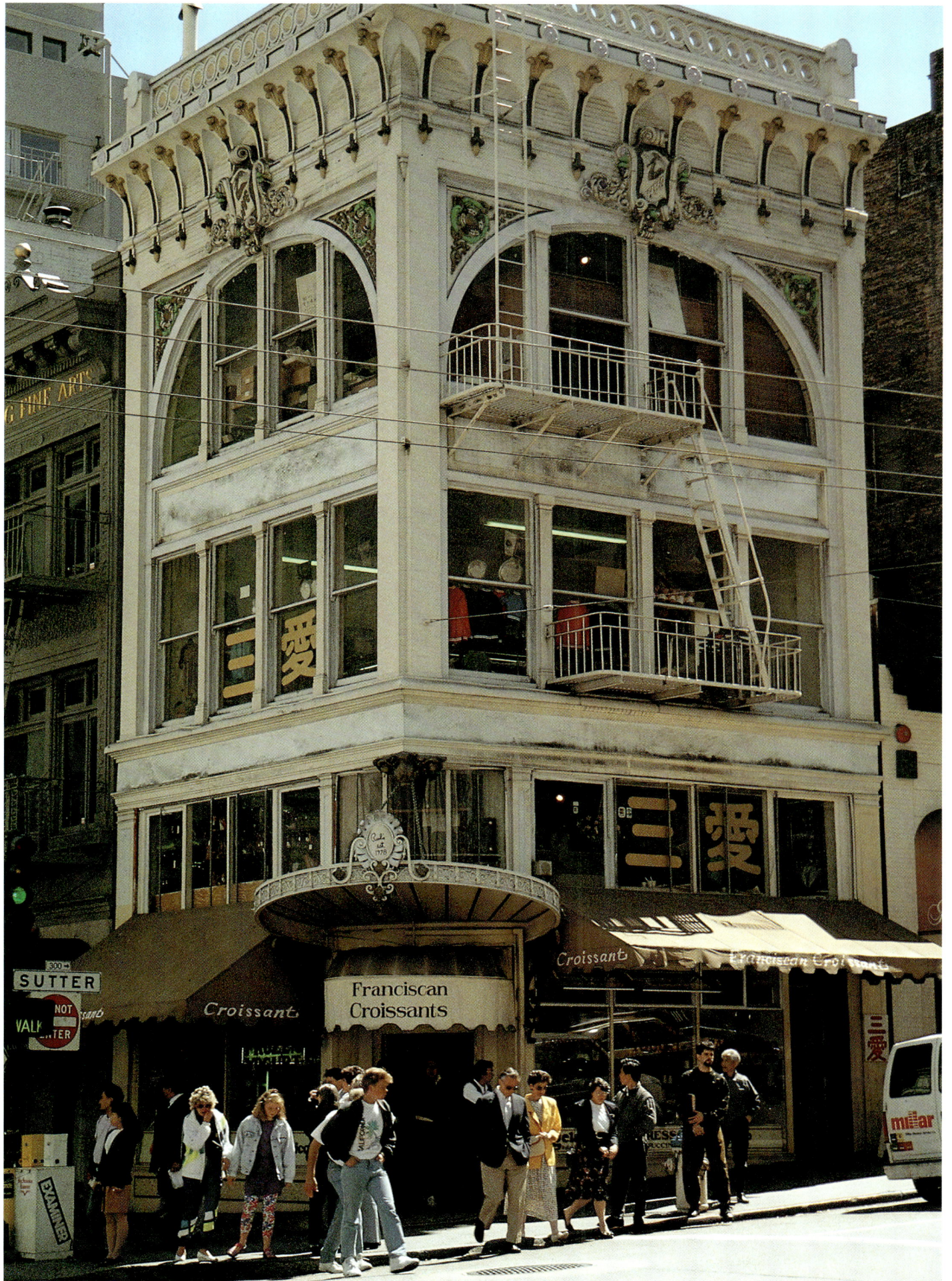

A light-hearted, elegant form of architecture which spills over into the street: the graceful lines of this glass-fronted historic office building (corner of Grant Avenue/Sutter Street) could make many a post-modern architect of today stand in amazement.

Huntington Park on Nob Hill with the Pacific Union Club, the most exclusive gentleman's club in town (centre).

For decades they have been a symbol of the city on the bay, dearly loved by the general public, hopelessly out of date and a form of transport that the citizens of San Francisco have more than once had to save from being scrapped.

THE CABLE CAR: A MONUMENT ON WHEELS

After World War II, the city council wanted to replace the cable cars with buses. But they had not reckoned with the citizens of San Francisco, who protested the idea. The cable cars were put on the protected list in 1964 and in 1982 sixty million

What could be finer than to rattle up and down the steep streets of San Francisco, standing half in a tram and half out, on the running board? We are, of course, talking about the cable cars, those magnificent, old-fashioned tram cars pulled by steel cables that the city of San Francisco still runs for the sake of the nostalgia they still awaken in tourists and residents alike.

It was Andrew Hallidie, who had manufactured steel cables during the years of the gold rush, who first thought up the idea of a cable car system in 1870. It was easy to construct and still functions perfectly today, one hundred-twenty years later. An endless steel cable runs under the surface of the street, the car rolling along the track above the cable has a claw arm which grips the cable, propelling into a controlled motion.

The first cable cars rolled down the steep slope of Clay Street in 1873. The system proved to be a success and soon a whole

Top left and centre: The lack of modern comfort cannot put off true cable car fans. Top right: Levers are used to drive and brake the cable cars. Centre: These huge drive wheels in the Cable Car Barn propel the steel ropes and therefore all the cable cars in the city. Bottom: Passengers also lend a hand to turn the cars.

network of tracks and cables spread over the city. Around the turn of the century there were around six hundred cars crossing San Francisco in all directions, on a network of tracks some 175 kilometres (109 miles) in length. In the following decades, however, the motor car gained the ascendency and gradually the cable car lines were closed.

dollars was spent on renovating the network. And so today the cars still roll up and down the hills at exactly ten miles (six kilometres) an hour, just as they have always done.

There are three lines still in service: California Street, Powell/Hyde and Powell/Mason. The cable under the longest of these, the California Street line, is a good 6.5 kilometres (four miles) long and has to be replaced every eight to ten months. In the Cable Car Museum, visitors can learn about the history of system. Corner of Washington/Mason Street, open daily 10.00 am to 5.00 pm.

Karl Teuschl

A form of public transport which is on the protected list – the cable car. Nobody will leave San Francisco without having at least once rattled their way over the city's hills: on the Powell-Mason line, which runs via Union Square (top left) and ends just before Fisherman's Wharf; on the Powell-Hyde line, which offers a view of Alcatraz from the junction Hyde/Lombard Street (top right); or on the California Street line, which runs over Nob Hill (bottom).

exhibitions of the nineteenth century. In spite of the war being waged in Europe the exhibition attracted millions of visitors. Twenty-four years later there was yet another exhibition, the Golden Gate International Exposition, which was held to celebrate the completion of the Oakland Bay Bridge in 1936 as well as the opening of Joseph Strauss' Golden Gate Bridge in 1937. Both bridges are triumphs of technology, famous all over the world. But the Golden Gate Bridge has the privilege of being the symbol of San Francisco.

An event of great importance for the whole world took place in San Francisco from 25 April to 25 June 1945. It was an international conference which came to an official end in the opera house on 24 June 1945, the climax being the acceptance of the United Nations Charter. As the United Nations building was later built in New York, few people remember that the United Nations organization was founded in San Francisco.

A Splendid Setting

Even though San Francisco grew more and more respectable as the years passed, it was not spared the problems facing any city undergoing the process of modernization and a dramatic population influx. A clear indication of the continuous struggle against crime lay only two kilometres (just over one mile) off the shore of San Francisco in the bay: the island of Alcatraz.

The shudder that runs down the spine of anyone visiting Alcatraz today, something which has been possible since 1973, is caused by the history of this former prison and memories which are much more real within the walls. The novelists who have created their own special brand of detective stories, using the atmosphere of San Francisco, have also tried to cause just the same sort of shudder.

But of course, the city really comes into its own when it is used as the setting for films, both for the big screen and television. There is a wealth of themes to choose from, from the wild days long gone through to the more problematic modern times. "Flame of the Barbary Coast" by Joe Kane, Howard Hawks' "Barbary Coast" and "The San Francisco Story" by Robert Parrish all have as their main ideas the days of the gold rush and the cleansing by vigilantes.

The film "San Francisco", which was produced in 1936, was a shattering experience from several points of view. Under the direction of W.S. Van Dyke, Clark Gable, Jeanette Macdonald, Spencer Tracy, Jack Holt and other less well-known actors "re-lived" the 1906 earthquake. John Hoffmann's special effects, created especially for the film, made the earthquake seem so threateningly realistic that they were considered unsurpassable for many years; many individual scenes from the film were re-used in entirely different films.

John Huston's film "The Sign of the Falcon", one of the most important films of its genre, was the screen version of Dashiell Hammett's novel "The Maltese Falcon". With Humphrey Bogart as Sam Spade a whole new style was created in this film. The scene is set from the beginning with a few shots of the Golden Gate Bridge, making the immediately connection between the atmosphere of the story and the city of San Francisco. On the other hand, many inside shots in the course of the film put the story on a more general footing so that it is not necessarily typical of San Francisco.

The view to the east from the highest point of Hyde Street towards Lombard Street, with the famous bends (foreground) leading to Telegraph Hill and Coit Tower.

After World War II producers of crime films used the city increasingly as a picturesque setting, for example Don Siegel in "The Lineup", John Boorman in "Point Blank", Alfred Hitchcock in "Vertigo", Peter Yates in "Bullitt" and Walter Hill in "48 Hours".

Comedies such as Peter Bogdanovitch's "What's Up, Doc?", musicals such as Anthony Mann's "Glenn Miller Story" and melodramas such as Sydney Lanfield's "The Well-Groomed Bride" prove that there is more than crime going on in San Francisco. Stanley Kramer's "Guess Whose Coming to Dinner" highlights the town's racial problem. And finally, in his film "My Favourite Brunette", Elliot Nugent parodies "The Sign of the Falcon" with Bob Hope portraying detective Sam Spade.

Television has also grasped the opportunity to turn both San Francisco's past and present into earnings. "Wells Fargo" was a western series in which Jim Hardie represented the interests of the well-known company from the main office in San Francisco. "Barbary Coast" was a short-lived attempt to mix the adventures of the wild west with the spy scene. But it was the series "Have Gun, Will Travel" which came closest to capturing for the television screen the atmosphere of days gone by, the combination of wild impetuosity and fine culture.

The nine sharp bends with a drop of forty percent at the Russian Hill end of Lombard Street between Hyde and Leavenworth are a major attraction for tourists who visit the city by car. And the tourist on foot will also enjoy the sight of the magnificent terraces carpeted with flowers.

Chinatown, with 80,000 residents the largest Chinese community outside of China. Here a view of Jackson Street.

平園餅家

火關聖戲院

HUNAN HOME'S

TI SUN

江南海鮮店 Chung King RESTAURANT

JACKSON PAULTO

New MAXIN

PING YU RESTAUR

湖南又一村

鋦鐽 油漆 RESTAUR

GREAT ST THEATER

L'AMOU 78

LIVE ENTERTAINMENT L'AMOUR CLUB DANCING NIGHTLY

樂隊 L'AMOUR

$

"Ironside" and, perhaps moreso, "The Streets of San Francisco", provided viewers with an impressive picture of the city as well as good entertainment for years.

The earthquake of 1989 was also treated in an unspectacular but sensitive fashion in the weekly television series "Night Falcon". In the episode entitled "San Francisco, 17 October 1989" it was not the damage caused by the earthquake that was the focal point, but rather the human side to the story, the feeling the everyone was in the same predicament and had to help each other in the days following the quake that was the storyline.

San Francisco's Chinatown: one big market with exotic vegetables and fruit, displaying the culinary diversity of the home country on the far side of the Pacific.

Music, Flower Power and the Underground

Music has always been important in San Francisco, with classical and modern existing harmoniously side by side. Sometimes they even intermingle, for example when classical music takes on gigantic proportions otherwise known only in the context of the pop scene: famous tenor Luciano Pavarotti attracted 25,000 people to an open-air concert in Golden Gate Park.

On a smaller scale, there are also parallels to be drawn with the cultural life of other big cities. For example, San Francisco has a boys' choir, just like Vienna; founded in 1948, the San Francisco Boys' Choir is one of the most famous choirs in the United States.

The city on the bay later developed into a distinctive centre of pop music. When young people began to take to the streets in the 1960's to show their opposition to the lifestyle of the time, it was the picture of San Francisco created by the media that attracted the flower children almost as if by magic to the town on the bay, whether to smoke marijuana in their Yerba Buena, live their own alternative way of life, work as artists, or make music. They came to, and stayed in, San Francisco to live their own lives.

Scott McKenzie just happened to be a musician who made his break just at the right moment to market the feeling prevalent on the scene. Groups such as the Grateful Dead or Jefferson Airplane played a much more important role from a musical point of view. Joan Baez, the protest singer, also came from the Bay Area. Otis Redding's "Sittin' on the Dock of the Bay" still rings in our ears and who can forget Tony Bennett singing "High on a hill it calls to me, where little cable cars climb half-way to the stars …". Without the influences emanating from San Francisco, pop music would certainly be a lot less developed today.

Compared with the young people's rebellion in the 1960's, their forerunner, the relatively-small beat generation of the late 1950's, was a mere rustling of leaves in the wind. The new sub-culture, which liked to call itself an underground culture, affected society much more deeply, branched off in various directions and gained a hold in many different fields.

Unlike many Chinese people in San Francisco, who maintain the traditional way of dressing and the habits of their origins, this man on Grant Avenue is dressed like a modern American businessman.

26

On Grant Avenue in the heart of San Francisco, there's very little to remind us that this is the United States. In addition to the many restaurants specializing in the different regional cuisines of China, Chinatown has all the hustle and bustle typical of an Asian trading centre.

For example, many new publications which reflected the new trends appeared on the scene in those years including underground comics such as Gary Arlington's "San Francisco Comic Book" and the committed journalism of "Rolling Stone" magazine, which developed out of San Francisco's music scene.

The activities of Gay Activism, on the other hand, are just the opposite of underground. Gay Activism is the movement of both, male and female homosexuals which developed in the liberal atmosphere of San Francisco before spreading throughout the country, drawing the public's attention to above all the problems of AIDS.

It's All Things to All People

This myth called San Francisco exercises a magnetic attraction. The city charms everyone with its cosmopolitan air and makes them feel at home. Or as the singer Chi Coltrane explained, you can be a newcomer to San Francisco, but you will never a stranger.

And anyone who has been to San Francisco will have a story to tell. Only recently a former classmate was saying what a pity it was that Chinatown would probably soon lose its special charm, because it was being deliberately allowed to run down to a noticeable degree by the residents in order to deter the Hong Kong refugees expected to arrive in the next few years. Many Hong Kong citizens

have in the last number of years bought sizeable amounts of property in the district in preparation of their island's reversion to Chinese control. San Francisco will no doubt come to terms with this problem as it already has with so many others.

The first story I ever heard about San Francisco from a visitor to the city was of a more cheerful nature. It was told to me by my school's music teacher, Munich composer Karl Meister, whose Christmas Oratorio was first performed in San Francisco in 1962. He spoke about the remarkable cable cars, the charming sights of the city, the magnificent view of the sea and the surprises the climate had in store. Owing to the mildness of the weather he had disregarded his host's warning to take his raincoat with him when he went out one day. He returned soaking wet because a sudden swirl of fog had showered him with spray. And, perhaps, it is the fog which, in the end, is the reason why San Francisco has become one of the world's dream cities. Fog-bound localities always have something mysterious about them: one minute they are bathed in bright sunlight, the next they have completely disappeared from view.

Hardly do we feel we know the place when it surprises with some new relevation, thus forcing us to keep an active and open mind. This applies particularly to San Francisco, of which someone once said, "It's all things to all people". San Francisco does not merely offer something for everyone, it offers everything for everyone.

A friend of mine's sister has developed a long-standing relationship with the city after first visiting it at the completion of her university studies. "It's just beautiful, just beautiful," she says. Though the shops are somewhat expensive for her, she pays the prices because the goods are unique and anything you could want to buy is offered. She enjoys the art scene, for San Francisco is a respected centre of music, theatre, literature and the creative arts.

But she admits she is drawn to the city because of its people. "It's an eye-opening city, everybody goes there." Though she's never ridden the cable cars, people-watching on Fisherman's Wharf is her favorite activity. You can see the latest dances on the promenade here before they become trends. In amongst the people out for a walk will be street artists of every conceivable variety as well as Vietnam veterans in uniform. Among her memories is one of encountering movie director Steven Spielberg while shopping one afternoon. Dressed in jeans and a baseball cap, he had trouble convincing the sales-clerk that he had enough money to cover his purchase. In comparison to other big cities, San Francisco may be trendy but not upscale for as she comments, "everyone is here together, there is a great sense of community." With this in mind, then, who will be surprised to hear that Rudyard Kipling once said "It's hard to leave San Francisco."

There's very little left to remind us of the original fishing harbour of the Italian immigrants, except for the boats and fish restaurants. Fisherman's Wharf is now an attraction for those looking for a touch of maritime nostalgia.

You can get any-
thing from cookies
to pizzas, from live
oysters (with pearl)
to modern artistic
t-shirts on Pier 39,
an amusement
centre on the his-
torical pier, con-
verted in 1978. In
the background
are Coit Tower
(left) and the
Transamerica
Pyramid.

AN AMERICAN DREAM CITY
Accounts and Descriptions of San Francisco

A European city in America? A gateway to the Orient? A utopia by the sea? Of San Francisco only one thing is certain: in no other American city is there such a lively mix of people and cultures living in such close proximity to one another. The greatest problem for visitors is finding enough time to explore the sights of the city as well as the surrounding countryside. The texts included here were written by visitors and residents of San Francisco over the last one hundred and fifty years.

The Mission Frontier

Each mission has allotted to it, in the first instance, a tract of land of about fifteen miles square, which is generally fertile and well suited for husbandry. This land is set apart for the general uses of the mission, part being cultivated, and part left in its natural condition and occupied as grazing ground. The buildings of the mission are, like the Presidio, all on the same general plan, but are varied according to the locality and number of the inhabitants. Most of the missionary villages or residences are surrounded by a high wall enclosing the whole; others have no such protection but consist of open rows of streets of little huts built of bricks: some of these are tiled and whitewashed and look neat and comfortable; others are dirty and in disrepair and in every way uncomfortable. In the mission of Santa Clara, which in several respects excels the others, the houses of the Indians form five rows or streets, which compared with the old straw huts must be considered really comfortable: and this is the greatest improvement that has taken place in the domestic civilization of these people at the missions. The buildings are generally built in the form of a square or part of a square, the church usually forming a portion of the elevation. The apartments of the fathers, which are often spacious, the granaries and workshops compose the remainder. The Indian population generally live in huts at about two hundred yards distant from the principal edifices; these huts are sometimes made of *adobes*, but the Indians are often left to raise them on their own plan; viz. of rough poles erected into a conical figure, of about four yards in circumference at the base, covered with dry grass and a small aperture for the entrance. When the huts decay, they set them on fire, and erect new ones; which is only the work of a day. In these huts the married part of the community live, the unmarried of both sexes being kept, each sex separate, in large barn-like apartments, where they work under strict supervision. The storehouses and workshops, at some of the larger missions, are of great extent and variety. There may be seen a place for melting tallow, one for making soap, workshops for smiths, carpenters, &c., storehouses for the articles manufactured, and the produce of the farms: viz. stores for tallow, soap, butter, salt, wool, hides, wheat, peas, beans, &c. &c. &c. Four or five soldiers have their residence a few yards further off, and are meant to watch the Indians, and to keep order; but they are generally lazy, idle fellows; and often give the missionary more trouble than all his Indians; and instead of rendering assistance increase his troubles. But in all Spanish countries, nothing can possibly be done without soldiers, and the idea of having any public establishment without a guard of soldiers would appear quite ridiculous.

The church is, of course, the main object of attraction at all the missions, and is often gaudily decorated. In some of the missions where there is good building-stone in the vicinity, the external appearance of the sacred building is not unseemly; in other missions the exterior is very rude. In all of them the interior is richer than the outside promises. In several there are pictures, and the subject of these is generally representations of heaven or hell, glaringly coloured purposely to strike the rude senses of the Indians. Pérouse says that the picture of hell in the church of San Carlos has, in this way, done incalculable service in promoting conversion; and well remarks that the protestant mode of worship, which forbids images and pompous ceremonies, could not make any progress among these people. He is of opinion that the picture of paradise in the same church, has exerted comparatively little effect on account of its tameness: but Langsdorff tells of wonders in this way wrought by a figure of the virgin represented as

30

Continued on page 36

Most of San Francisco's houses are of wood, due to the danger of earthquakes. Brick buildings like this one in the antiques district around Jackson Square (Hotaling Street) are rare. A great contrast is provided by the hypermodern architecture of the Transamerica Pyramid.

Individual tastes have triumphed when it comes to the outer appearance of the houses below Twin Peaks.

THE GOLDEN GATE

The completion of the thirteen kilometre (eight mile) long San Francisco-Oakland Bay Bridge and the impending opening of the Golden Gate Bridge, built between 1933 and 1937 to plans by Joseph B. Strauss, were both celebrated in 1936 with the Golden Gate International Exposition. It is, however, the Golden Gate Bridge which has the privilege of being the symbol of San Fran-

New York harbour was completed in 1964, this represented the longest distance between two bridge supports; even the more modern bridge in New York has supports which are only eighteen metres (fifty-nine feet) further apart. If you compare the thirty-five million dollars it cost

strong because of the difference in the tides between the open sea and the bay. As the bridge is open to pedestrians, on the second level, as well as cars, it was inevitable that it would attract not only tourists but also those tired of life.
The Golden Gate Bridge is probably one of the most photographed bridges in the world, in spite of the fact that it is often veiled in fog. The high humidity in the air

makes it necessary for the bridge to be checked constantly for corrosion and repainted. Red lead protects the bridge against rust but it is by no means unsusceptible to the rigours of the climate and so the bridge-painters have a job for life: before the painting has been completed at one end of the bridge it is time to start applying the next coat at the other end. And those painters certainly have a lot of steel to protect: 128,744 kilometres (eighty thousand miles) of steel wire in the two main support cables alone.

Wolfgang J. Fuchs

cisco. It is also considered to be one of the seven wonders of the modern world owing to its daring construction.
It is 2.8 kilometres (1.7 miles) long and runs from the northernmost point of San Francisco across the two kilometre (just over one mile) entrance to San Francisco Bay, continuing on to Sausalito in Marin County. The two red pylons which carry the weight of the bridge with the help of the two main support cables are 227 metres (745 feet) high and stand 1,280 metres (4,199 feet) apart. Until the Verrazano Narrows Bridge at the entrance to

The bridge today (top) and on 27 May 1937 (centre). Bottom: Joseph B. Strauss.

to build the Golden Gate Bridge with the 305 million dollars spent on the Verrazano Narrows Bridge, it is obvious just how much the construction costs increased in thirty-five years.
The completion of the bridge in only four years was a particularly difficult task as the foundations for each of the two pylons had to be laid in water which was constantly on the move. Further, the current near the Golden Gate Bridge is extremely

The National
Maritime Museum
and Aquatic Park
provide informa-
tion about the his-
tory of seafaring
and its import-
ance for the west
coast of America.
A visit to the
museum ships
moored here is
particularly
interesting.

Less famous than
the Golden Gate
Bridge, but an
equally impressive
example of bridge
building is the San
Francisco-Oak-
land Bay Bridge. It
is 13.3 kilometres
(8.3 miles) long,
has two levels and
links, via Treasure
Island (left in the
picture), San
Francisco and
Oakland. The
lower level carries
traffic to Oakland,
the upper level
carries the traffic
to San Francisco.

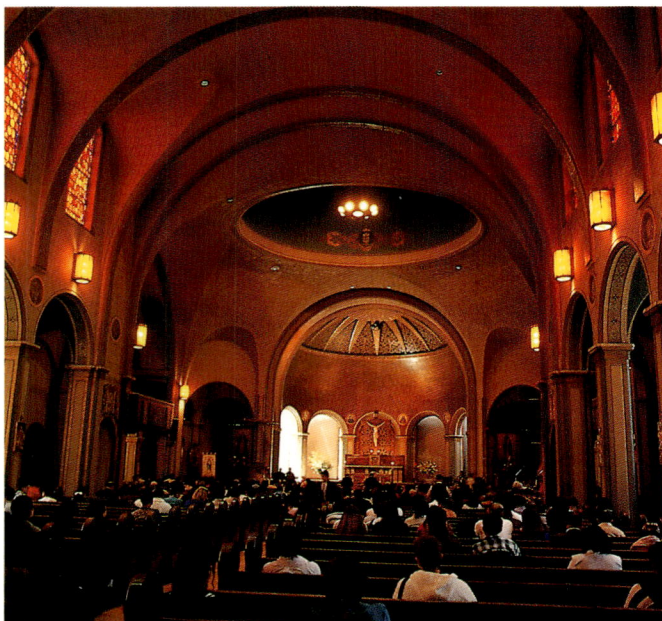

springing from the coronal of leaves of the *Agave Americana*, or great American aloe, instead of the ordinary stem! The priests also take care to be provided with rich dresses for the same purpose of inspiring awe.

A British visitor ALEXANDER FORBES wrote this description of California's missions in 1839, at a time when the Indians were gradually receding from the missionary territory.

The Great Quake

A month afterward I enjoyed my first earthquake. It was one which was long called the "great" earthquake, and is doubtless so distinguished till this day. It was just after noon, on a bright October day. I was coming down Third Street. The only objects in motion anywhere in sight in that thickly-built and populous quarter, were a man in a buggy behind me, and a street car wending slowly up the cross street. Otherwise, all was solitude and a Sabbath stillness. As I turned the corner, around a frame house, there was a great rattle and jar, and it occurred to me that here was an item! – no doubt a fight in that house. Before I could turn and seek the door, there came a really terrific shock; the ground seemed to roll under me in waves, interrupted by a violent joggling up and down, and there was a heavy grinding noise as of brick houses rubbing together. I fell up against the frame house and hurt my elbow. I knew what it was, now, and from mere reportorial instinct, nothing else, took out my watch and noted the time of day; at that moment a third and still severer shock came, and as I reeled about on the pavement trying to keep my footing, I saw a sight! The entire front of a tall four-story brick building in Third Street sprung outward like a door and fell sprawling across the street, raising a dust like a great volume of smoke! And here came the buggy – overboard went the man, and in less time than I can tell it the vehicle was distributed in small fragments along three hundred yards of street. One could have fancied that somebody had fired a charge of chair-rounds and rags down the thoroughfare. The street car had stopped, the horses were rearing and plunging, the passengers were pouring out at both ends, and one fat man had crashed half way through a glass window on one side of the car, got wedged fast and was squirming and screaming like an impaled madman. Every door of every house, as far as the eye could reach, was vomiting a stream of human beings; and almost before one could execute a wink and begin another, there was a massed multitude of people stretching in endless procession down every street my position commanded. Never was solemn solitude turned into teeming life quicker.

Of the wonders wrought by "the great earthquake," these were all that came under my eye; but the tricks it did, elsewhere, and far and wide over the town, made toothsome gossip for nine days. The destruction of property

Top and centre: Mission Dolores, founded in 1776 by the Franciscan monk Junipero Serra, is the oldest building in the city. It was built largely by Indians and was intended as a centre for the Christianization of the natives. The pattern of Indian woven baskets can still be seen on the ceiling.

Bottom: In 1918 a huge basilica was built beside the old mission, with a small museum in one of the side rooms.

Top: The heart of Little Italy on Washington Square. Marilyn Monroe and baseball star Joe DiMaggio were married in the Church of Saint Peter and Paul.

Centre: The California Palace of the Legion of Honour is a museum devoted exclusively to French art. A copy of Rodin's "Thinker" stands in the inner courtyard of the building.

Bottom: The Exploratorium, an exemplary museum of science and technology, is housed in the palace of Fine Arts.

was trifling – the injury to it was widespread and somewhat serious. The "curiosities" of the earthquake were simply endless. Gentleman and ladies who were sick, or were taking a siesta, or had dissipated till a late hour and were making up lost sleep, thronged into the public streets in all sorts of queer apparel, and some without any at all. One woman who had been washing a naked child, ran down the street holding it by the ankles as if it were a dressed turkey. Prominent citizens who were supposed to keep the Sabbath strictly, rushed out of saloons in their shirt-sleeves, with biiliard cues in their hands. Dozens of men, with necks swathed in napkins, rushed from barbers' shops, lathered to the eyes or with one cheek clean shaved and the other still bearing a hairy stubble. Horses broke from stables, and a frightened dog rushed up a short attic ladder and out on to a roof, and when his scare was over had not the nerve to go down again the same way he had gone up. A prominent editor flew downstairs, in the principal hotel, with nothing on but one brief under-garment – met a chambermaid, and exclaimed:

"Oh, what *shall* I do? Where shall I go?"

She responded with naïve serenity:

"If you have no choice, you might try a clothing store!"

A certain foreign consul's lady was the acknowledged leader of fashion, and every time she appeared in anything new or extraordinary, the ladies in the vicinity made a raid on their husband's purses and arrayed themselves similarly. One man who had suffered considerably and growled accordingly, was standing at the window when the shocks came, and the next instant the consul's wife, just out of the bath, fled by with no other apology for clothing than – a bath towel! The sufferer rose superior to the terrors of the earthquake, and said to his wife:

"Now *that* is something *I like*! Get out your towel, my dear!"

The plastering that fell from ceilings in San Francisco that day would have covered several acres of ground. For some days afterward, groups of eyeing and pointing men stood about many a building, looking at long zigzag cracks that extended from the eaves to the ground. Four feet of the tops of three chimneys on one house were broken square off and turned around in such a way as to completely stop the draught. A crack a hundred feet long gaped open six inches wide in the middle of one street, and then shut together again with such force as to ridge up the meeting earth like a slender grave. A lady, sitting in her rocking and quaking parlour, saw the wall part at the ceiling, open and shut twice, like a mouth, and then drop the end of a brick on the floor like a tooth. She was a woman easily disgusted with foolishness, and she arose and went out of there. One lady who was coming downstairs was astonished to see a bronze Hercules lean forward on its pedestal as if to strike her with its club. They both reached

the bottom of the flight at the same time, – the woman insensible from the fright. Her child, born some little time afterwards, was club-footed. However – on second thought – if the reader see any coincidence in this, he must do it at his own risk.

This excerpt is taken from MARK TWAIN's (1835 – 1910) 1906 work "The Innocents at Home".

A Pacific Coast Lighthouse ...

"It's the last manned light station on the Pacific Coast," Herk Schuber said. "It's also one of the oldest lighthouses

still in use on this coast. And incidentally, it's the only one in the United States, I'm told, that's reached by a suspension bridge."

As second in command of the Coast Guard's Point Bonita Light Station, Machinery Technician Second Class Schuber was in charge on the sunny September day of my visit. Everyone understood this except Lance, a rambunctious young Doberman pinscher with a marked tendency toward insubordination. With Herk, Lance, and Coast Guardsman George Thomas, I set out on the ten-minute walk to the light from the station's main cluster of buildings. Herk answered my questions between fierce commands aimed at Lance as the dog dashed off in one direc-

tion, then another to investigate the brushy hillside. The path wound through the dry chaparral, much of the time affording a clear view back across the Golden Gate to the shining white skyline of San Francisco. Finally we made our way through a tunnel and across the footbridge to the sheer tip of the rocky point. There, its cylindrical lantern room offset above a larger building, stood the venerable lighthouse. "The first light was built in 1855 up on the hill, where the radar is now," Herk said. "But it wasn't a satisfactory site – too high above the fog – so in 1857 they moved it here, with the lantern about 130 feet above the water. The year before, the West Coast's first sound signal was installed; it was a cannon fired every 30 minutes when the fog was in."

Today a foghorn can be turned on from the station headquarters, and the light operates automatically. "But we still pull duty at the lighthouse because, for the time being at least, it's a key weather-watching post for the entrance to San Francisco Bay," Herk said.

Nevertheless, the days of this last manned light station apparently are numbered. Sometime in 1979 the Coast Guard expects to have in place the intricate electronic equipment that will enable Point Bonita to go to fully automated status.

"Most of the time, things are pretty dull," Herk said. "But when there's a storm, this can be an exciting place. We get drenching spray from the waves up here, even though the control room is 115 feet above the sea."

As we climbed about the solid old structure, George Thomas showed me the beautiful Fresnel lens that magnifies a 1,000-watt bulb – or, for that matter, a kerosene lamp, as in past years – into a beam rated at a million candlepower and visible 18 miles at sea.

On the way back, I was struck again by the contrast between the city just across the Golden Gate and the quiet, natural scene around us. As if to reinforce the point, Lance flushed a yearling doe from the brush. With a shout Herk brought the dog to heel, then watched the deer bound down the steep hillside, leap gracefully over a stream-bed, and disappear from view.

In conjunction with the National Geographic Society, MERRILL WINDSOR travelled throughout California.

This impressive monument in Golden Gate Park is to the memory of Francis Scott Key (1779 – 1843), the man who wrote the American national anthem.

... and the Golden Gate Bridge

For the opening, May 27 to June 13, 1937, poppies had been sown on both approaches to the bridge, and they blazed their golden welcome to the party to which all the West, Canada, and Mexico had been invited. Schools were closed for the celebration. The bridge was opened to pedestrians on May 27 before vehicles were allowed. Thousands dashed over, some skating and some on stilts, others wheeling babies.

39

Golden Gate Park: the Conservatory of Flowers, a magnificent greenhouse in the Victorian style.

Early in the day Governor Merriam, Mayor Rossi, and guest governors crossed the bay to participate in the dedication ceremonies on the Marin side. Two huge redwoods were thrown across the highway as barriers, but three champion woodsmen swiftly sawed them in two. "Kindly remove the obstruction," ordered Governor Merriam. "Long may this approach serve him who would reach the other side. May it always be a happy crossing."

Again chains were severed. In the first southbound car was Dean Kintner, the district engineer, who fell from the high approach viaduct on the final day of riveting. "I got banged up in that fall but, golly, this was worth it!"

The electric moment came. President Roosevelt at Washington gave the green-light signal. ... Shouts of people on the sidewalk drowned the sound of 500 planes soaring overhead from Admiral Hepburn's fleet of 122 ships – cannon boomed. Acetylene torches burned ima-

ginary chains at the North Tower as the car containing Mayor Rossi and Governor Merriam moved forward. President Filmer of the Golden Gate Bridge and Highway District severed the gold chain; Mayor Rossi, the silver; Frank P. Doyle, treasurer of the Empire Redwood Association, the copper. At the beautiful floral gate Chief Engineer Strauss formally presented the bridge to the public. "The bridge needs no encomium, neither praise nor eulogy, it speaks for itself."

Queen Empress Vivian Sorenson of San Francisco, assisted by ladies in waiting, opened the floral gates. Admiral Hepburn's capital ships moved beneath the bridge into the harbor. The Chilean battleship led visiting foreign vessels. Mrs. Ethel Olson, of 40 Capistrano Street, paid the first official toll. Francis Terry was led over by a seeing-eye dog. Seven-year-old Margaret Little of El Cerrito crashed the gate, and 32,000 automobiles crossed the first day.

At Bal Tabarin there was a luncheon for a thousand guests. In the streets were men from the fleet, cowboys in ten-gallon hats, Mexicans in sombreros and serapes, and cave girls from Oregon clothed only in wolfskins. In the parade there were 150 floats. A ball was held at the Civic Auditorium for the families of the eleven workers who lost their lives building the bridge, and memorial exercises for them were held on Crissy Field. President Ubrico sent a giant marimba from Guatemala. Twenty-six-year-old Bernardine King flew up from Los Angeles and risked discipline by darting her black and yellow biplane under the bridge. In Polk Gulch an up-to-date Joaquin Murietta, in costume, staged holdups.

Night brought a gorgeous pageant to Crissy Field: Wilbur Hall's *The Land of Gold* presented on a 300-foot stage with redwood grove background. On bleachers, 20,000 people listened while John Charles Thomas sang the leading male role. Climaxing the last scene, the bridge itself was flooded with blazing rockets shooting upward.

This description of the opening of the Golden Gate Bridge was written by CORA OLDER, the wife of a prominent San Francisco newspaper editor.

Tristesse doesn't stand a chance when brilliant blue shades can even be found in front of a huge garage in Fulton Street.

Cable Car Rules

1. NEVER attempt to get off or on a Car while it is moving. NEVER run after a Car or in front of one. ALWAYS step off a Car in the direction of travel. WATCH for passing autos and Cable Cars.

2. ALWAYS hold on tight, even when the Car is stopped.

3. NEVER lean out or play around a Car.

4. NEVER touch, hold or grab the cords, levers, or other apparatus on a Car.

5. DO NOT stand behind the Gripman (the driver). ALWAYS keep doorways, exits, and work areas clear at all times, and as requested by the Conductor or Gripman; don't argue, please.

6. ALWAYS cooperate with requests from Car personnel; their jobs are to ensure a safe, pleasant ride for you, and their job is not an easy one. Cable Cars can be dangerous, so please heed the Gripman and Conductor and help to reduce accidents and stress.

7. HAVE your fare, ticket, or transfer ready for the Conductor when he or she asks for it. DO NOT try to change large bills on the Car. The current basic adult fare is $ 1.00. Consult Cable crews or other MUNI personnel for current rates, transfer regulations, round-trip ticket information, etc. Call 673-MUNI or ask at your hotel.

8. NEVER rush, push or shove when boarding or leaving a Car; be especially considerate of elderly passengers and children. DO NOT try to force your way onto an obviously overcrowded Car. Note: Full cars will not stop to pick up passengers.

The strict sym-
metry of the façade
of this building on
the corner of Polk
and Bay Streets is
broken only by the
typical zig-zag of
the fire-escape.

43

The famous view of Downtown San Francisco over the Victorian houses in Steiner Street on Alamo Square.

Downtown San Francisco as seen through the Golden Gate Bridge from Marine Headlands. The northern support of the bridge is in the foreground left.

9. ALWAYS hold onto small children, and PAY ATTENTION to what is happening around you. LOOK, and be careful.

10. IF YOU ARE DRIVING while in The City, remember that Cable Cars, like pedestrians, have the right of way *at all times*. ALWAYS YIELD. NEVER get in front of a Car on a hill or block the tracks everywhere, and if you hear a Cable Car bell clanging behind you, *get out of the way*. Be extremely careful when passing a Car. DON'T SPEED PLEASE.

11. Transfers and tickets can allow you to get on and off a Car without paying another fare. Ask your Conductor or Gripman to explain how they work.

12. Oh, and NEVER call a Cable Car a trolley …

These basic cable car regulations and safety rules were included in a recent guide to San Francisco.

The City's Drivers

A pile of miscellaneous articles was found heaped up at a late hour last night away down somewhere in Harrison street, which attracted the notice of numbers of passers-by, and divers attempts were made to analyze the same without effect, for the reason that no one could tell where to begin, or which was on top. Two Special Policemen dropped in just then and solved the difficulty, showing a clean inventory of one horse, one buggy, two men and an indefinite amount of liquor. The liquor couldn't be got at to be gauged, consequently the proof of it couldn't be told; the men, though, were good proof that the liquor was there, for they were as drunk as Bacchus and his brother.

A fight had been on hand somewhere, and one of the men had been close to it, for his face was painted up in various hues, sky-blue and crimson being prominent. The order of the buggy was inverted, and the horse beyond a realizing sense of his condition. The men went with some noise to the station-house, and the animal, with attachments, being set to rights, ambled off to a livery stable on Kearny street.

A man fell off his own dray – or rather it was a large truck-wagon – in Davis street, yesterday, and the fore wheels passed over his body. A bystander stopped the horses and they backed the same wheels over the man's body a second time; after which he crawled out, jumped on the wagon, muttered something about being "tired of sich d--d foolishness," and drove off before a surgeon could arrive to amputate him!

Between June and October 1864, MARK TWAIN (1835 – 1910) was employed by the city desk of the "San Francisco Daily Morning Call".

One of the main
facts contributing
to San Francisco's
particular flair is
that it has a special
location – at the
entrance to the
Bay. To the west lies
the seemingly end-
less Pacific Ocean
and to the south,
hinterland in the
true sense of the
word. Alcatraz is
in the background
of the photo.

Map of San Francisco showing the following labelled features:

Legend — SAN FRANCISCO
- Highway
- Cable Car
- Scenic Drive

0   N   1 km

Golden Gate Bridge · Fort Point · Golden Gate National Recreation Area · Golden Gate Promenade · Fisherman's Wharf · Pier 39 · Aquatic Park · Golden Gate National Recreation Area · The Cannery · Jefferson Street · Fort Mason Center · National Maritime Museum · Ghirardelli Square · North Point St. · Telegraph Hill · Palace of Fine Arts · Mason Street · Marina Boulevard · Beach Street · Bay Street · Francisco Street · Chestnut Street · NORTH BEACH · Lombard Street · MARINA · Richardson Ave. · Lincoln Ave. · Lombard Street · Greenwich Street · Filbert Street · Greenwich Street · Columbus Avenue · Grant Avenue · Kearny Street · Montgomery Street · Battery Street · Embarcadero St. · PRESIDIO · Webster Street · Union Street · Green Street · Vallejo Street · Broadway · Steiner Street · Scott Street · Gough Street · Taylor Street · Jones Street · Leavenworth St. · Powell Street · Bank of Canton · Embarcadero Center · Ferry Bldg. · San Francisco-Oakland Bay Bridge · PACIFIC HEIGHTS · Alta Plaza · Jackson Street · Washington Street · Lafayette Park · Franklin Street · Tin How Temple · NOB HILL · CHINATOWN · Transamerica Pyramid · Justin Herman Plaza · West Pacific Avenue · Jackson Street · Sacramento Street · California Street · Pine Street · Clay Street · Sacramento Street · Grace Cathedral · Drachen-tor · FINANCIAL DISTRICT · Hyatt Regency Hotel · Broderick Street · Scott Street · WESTERN ADDITION · Japan Center · Bush Street · Sutter Street · Post Street · Union Square · Sheraton Palace Hotel · RICHMOND · Lake Street · Clement Street · Geary Boulevard · Anza Street · Balboa Street · Cabrillo Street · Sutter Street · Post Street · Geary Boulevard · O'Farrell Street · Ellis Street · Turk Street · Geary Street · O'Farrell Street · Ellis Street · TENDERLOIN · San Francisco Centre · Howard Street · Folsom Street · Main Public Library · City Hall · Civic Center · SOUTH OF MARKET · Market Street · Opera House · Civic Auditorium · Alamo Square · HAYES VALLEY · 9th Street · China Basin · Rainbow Waterfall · De Young Museum · Conservatory · Japanese Tea Garden · Music Concourse · African Hall · Cal. Academy of Sciences · Temple of Music · Huntington Falls · Golden Gate Park · Stadium · Panhandle · Masonic Avenue · Fele Street · Olak Street · Haight Street · HAIGHT-ASHBURY · Fulton Street · Frederik Street · Lincoln Way · Irving Street · Kirkham Street · BUENA VISTA · 12th Avenue · 14th Avenue · 18th Avenue · 19th Avenue · 21st Avenue · Quintara Street · Rivera Street · Taraval Street · Portola Drive · Twin Peaks · Douglas Street · Castro Street · Church Street · Dolores Street · Market Street · 17th Street · 18th Street · MISSION · Mission Dolores · 16th Street · 17th Street · 18th Street · Mission Street · Valencia Street · South Van Ness Avenue · POTRERO · 23rd Street · 25th Street · 26th Street · 27th Street · 28th Street · Clipper Street · Army Street · Potrero Avenue · Bryant Street · 2nd Street · 3rd Street · 4th Street · 5th Street · 7th Street

Inset map: San Pablo Bay · San Rafael · San Pablo · El Cerrito · Sausalito · ALCATRAZ · Berkeley · Oakland · SAN FRANCISCO · San Bruno · PACIFIC · San Francisco Bay

GENERAL INFORMATION

LOCATION AND SIZE. San Francisco or "the city" as the residents fondly call their town, is situated in the northern part of California at the tip of a peninsula between the Pacific Ocean and San Francisco Bay. The municipal area comprises 120 square kilometres (46 square miles) of land and 212 square kilometres (82 square miles) of water. At the latest count the population figure stood at 724,000, more than half of whom are of European origin. Approximately ten percent of the population are Blacks, thirty percent are Asians and some thirteen percent are immigrants from Central and South America.

San Francisco is, in fact, the fourth largest city in California but if we include the entire suburban area around the bay, with its well over six million residents, and other towns including Oakland and San José, the Bay Area is the fourth largest urban area in the United States after New York, Los Angeles and Chicago.

ECONOMY. Whereas formerly there were many small factories for the food and textile industries located in San Francisco, the city today earns most of its income from service industries. Banks and trading

The warmest month is September, which is virtually free of fog and has an average daily high temperature of 20.5 degrees Celsius (68 degrees Fahrenheit). In January, the coldest month, the average temperature is 13.2 degrees Celsius (56 degrees Fahrenheit).

TIME ZONE. The whole of California lies in the Pacific Time Zone, which is nine hours behind Central European Time, meaning people in San Francisco are having lunch when it is nine o'clock in the evening in Central Europe. The same time difference prevails during daylight savings time, when the clocks are put forward by an hour in both Europe and the United States. Between the west and east coasts there is a three hour time difference.

Chinatown, an Asia (Minor) in the United States. This is Commercial Street, a typical shopping street.

organizations and, particularly in the southern part of the Bay Area, numerous computer firms all cluster together in the economic region of San Francisco Bay.

Its location in the far west of America makes the city an excellent outlet for the quickly-expanding trade with Asia. Tourism, however, is still the city's most important branch of industry.

CLIMATE AND TRAVEL SEASON. Situated as it is on the 37 degree north (latitude), San Francisco has a mild, sunny climate all year round, although in summer the cool sea currents and coastal fog result in frequent considerable drops in temperature.

INFORMATION

San Francisco Convention & Visitors Bureau
P. O. Box 429097, San Francisco, CA 94142. Provides city maps on written request and also a very useful book entitled "The San Francisco Book" (enclose $ 1 to cover postage and handling, post to Europe approximately six weeks).

Visitor Information Center
Hallidie Plaza, corner Market/Powell Street (lower floor), Tel.: 391-2000; open Monday to Friday, 9.00 am to 5.30 pm; Saturday, 9.00 am to 3.00 pm; Sunday, 10.00 am to 2.00 pm.

HOW TO GET THERE

All visitors to the United States from Europe need a valid passport. Only if you plan to stay longer than three months do you need a visa, which can be obtained from American consulates and embassies in your home country. In additon to your personal luggage you may take into the United States two hundred cigarettes or fifty cigars or two kilos of tobacco as well as one litre of wine/spirits and gifts to the value of one hundred dollars. The import of fresh food (fruit or meat) and plants is strictly forbidden.

Direct flights from Europe to San Francisco last approximately eleven hours. Flights with American airlines take a little longer as passengers have to change at one or other of the major airports in the United States but they are usually cheaper. The quickest route is via the northern states, for example with an American Airlines connection through Chicago.

SFO, San Francisco's international airport, lies approximately twenty-two kilometres (fourteen miles) to the south of the city and is the fifth largest in the United States with some thirteen hundred flights every day. SFO Airport Buses run every twenty minutes to the centre of town, for seven dollars per passenger. The smaller buses, the Supershuttle or Yellow Airport Shuttle for example, are only a little more expensive but much more comfortable and will, if required, call at individual hotels and other (private) addresses in the city.

TIPS FOR THE JOURNEY

MONEY. There are dollar notes with the values 1, 2, 5, 10, 20, 50 and 100 but be careful not to confuse them: they are all the same size and are all the same green colour. They differ on the front, where each one portrays a different statesman. It is advisable to travel with travellers' cheques (in US dollars) and a credit card (Eurocard, Visa etc.) and a small amount of cash. Travellers' cheques are accepted everywhere in hotels, shops and restaurants, with change given in cash. Eurocheques are usually not accepted and only the larger bank branches will exchange foreign currencies for dollars.

HEALTH INSURANCE. All foreign tourists are automatically treated as private patients, therefore, at extremely high rates. For this reason you should be prepared for emergencies and take out health insurance for countries abroad before your journey.

OPENING TIMES. Post offices and small shops are usually open weekdays from 9.00 am to 5.30 pm, shopping malls until 9.00 pm from Thursday to Saturday, as well as during the day on Sunday. Souvenir shops and boutiques on Fisherman's Wharf usually stay open every day until 10.00 pm in the summer months, sometimes until later. Supermarkets and drugstores are in general open daily until midnight, and depending on the location are sometimes open round the clock.

TRANSPORT

A car is superfluous in the centre of San Francisco. The city is a perfect paradise for pedestrians and the public transport system is excellent, if there are longer distances to be covered. *San Francisco MUNI* runs buses, trams and the famous cable cars and there is additionally the underground railway *BART (Bay Area Rapid Transit)* which links the towns on either side of the bay. One journey, with a transfer if necessary, costs eighty-five cents on the MUNI. The *cable cars*, a popular tourist attraction, are a little more expensive at two dollars.

Day tickets can be bought for six dollars in the Visitor Information Centre; a three-day ticket costs ten dollars, a seven-day ticket fifteen dollars. There is also a brochure

The cable car, a nostalgic means of transport.

available at the centre which claims that the public means of transport are the most interesting sight in San Francisco!

Top: The steep hills make skillful parking a necessity. Bottom: The ferry to Alcatraz.

Taxis are relatively cheap and to be recommended because of the difficulties of parking in the centre of the city. The basic rate is $ 1.90 for the first mile and $ 1.40 for every subsequent mile. There may be extra charges for late night services.

Rental cars are available at the airport and in the centre from all the big hire companies. But a car is really only necessary for a lengthy tour of the suburbs. Be careful when parking: because of the steepness of the streets it is obligatory to leave the car in gear with the handbrake on and the wheels turned toward the curb.

Overland buses of the various companies, including Greyhound and Trailways, start from the Transbay Terminal at the corner of Mission/First Street.

FERRIES AND BOAT TRIPS

Blue and Gold Fleet
Pier 39
Ferries to Oakland and Alameda; circular tours of the harbour lasting seventy-five minutes.

Golden Gate Ferries
Ferry Building
Ferries to Sausalito and Larkspur at the northern end of the bay.

Red and White Fleet
Pier 41 and 43½
Ferries to Sausalito, Tiburon, Angel Island and Vallejo as well as round-trip tours of the harbour lasting approximately forty-five minutes. Tours can also be booked to the prison island of Alcatraz.

ACCOMMODATION

Staying in San Francisco itself is not, of course, as cheap as staying in the surrounding countryside, but it is not nearly as expensive as New York. Obviously there are luxury hotels and hotels with a long tradition. However in the course of the last few years a number of old hotels have been renovated and turned into so-called *boutique hotels*, small, well-run establishments where a double room with all modern conveniences will cost between eighty and one hundred-thirty dollars a night.

The *San Francisco Lodging Guide*, which is published annually by the city's Visitors' Bureau, can be of great help when planning a stay in San Francisco. During the peak summer season, from May to the end of September, it is advisable to make hotel reservations in advance.

A few tips: the latest luxury hotel in San Francisco is the *Ritz Carlton* on the corner of California/Stockton Street (Tel.: 296-7465), beautifully situated between Nob Hill and Chinatown with prices beginning at one hundred-seventy-five dollars. The magnificent old grand hotels on Nob Hill, such as the *Fairmont Hotel* (950 Mason Street, Tel.: 772-5000) which is familiar from many films, are in roughly the same price range.

But what about the more reasonable boutique hotels. The *Kensington Park* (450 Post Street, Tel.: 788-6400, double room one hundred-twenty dollars), just around the corner from United Square, and the nearby *Galleria Park* (191 Sutter Street, Tel.: 781-3060, double room one hundred-twenty-five dollars) are both to be recommended.

Even more reasonable hotels and motels are to be found in the northwestern part of the city, along Lombard Street and around Market Street. To be recommended are the *Sheehan Hotel* (620 Sutter Street, Tel.: 775-6500, from fifty dollars for a double room), and the *Best Western Americana* (121 Seventh Street, Tel.: 626-0200, from sixty-seven dollars for a double room).

FOOD AND DRINK

With more than 4,600 restaurants in the city it is very difficult to know which to choose, particularly because the great variety of excellent foreign restaurants make dining out in San Francisco quite an experience. A dish very typical of San Francisco and one that can be recommended is *Cioppino*, a stew made of fresh crabs, fish and vegetables.

Among tourists the restaurants with a view are, of course, obviously popular. Enjoy the magnificent view of the bay from *McCormick & Kuleto's* (Ghirardelli Square), a distinguished fish restaurant, or the *Old Swiss House* (Pier 39).

Fashionable places including *Hamburger Mary's* (1582 Folsom Street) South of Market and the *Fog City Diner* (1300 Battery Street) provide classic American food: good hamburgers and milk shakes with the nostalgic quality of the 1950's. You can get a really good steak and enjoy an excellent Sunday brunch at *Lehr's Greenhouse* (740 Sutter Street).

Regarding foreign restaurants: the place to go for sushi is the *Sushi Boat Restaurant* (389 Geary Street); for French cuisine try the very expensive *Fleur de Lys* (777 Sutter Street); Indian food is served in the *Maharani* (1122 Post Street); the best Italian food is to be had in North Beach, including at *Basta Pasta* (1268 Grant Avenue) well into the night.

A Dim Sum brunch at the weekend in Chinatown is something which is particularly good. It is also very easy to order: the exotic dishes are pushed past the table on small trolleys and the customer merely has to point to what he would like to try. To be recommended are *Tung Fong* (808 Pacific Street) and *Hong Kong Teahouse* (835 Pacific Street).

A grand hotel steeped in tradition, the Fairmont Hotel on Nob Hill.

A word of advice: service charges are usually not included in the bill, so therefore it is customary to leave about fifteen percent of the cost of the meal on the table or add it to the sum charged to the credit card. Many better quality restaurants have a strict dress code, meaning that men should wear a jacket and a tie, jeans on either sex are not welcomed. In many of the more popular restaurants it is also wise to reserve a table in advance.

The San Francisco Book, available from the Visitors Information Centre, has a detailed list of restaurants.

IN THE EVENING

San Francisco's oldest entertainment district is North Beach, the former seamen's

Anyone interested in antiques will feel at home in Jackson Square.

quarter. It extends around the junction of Columbus Avenue and Broadway, with neon signs to tempt the unsuspecting into strip clubs. In spite of this element, however, there are still one or two pubs in the district which have retained something of the old San Francisco style. The *Tosca* (242 Columbus Avenue) is a meeting-place for trendy cappuccino drinkers, while *Vesuvio's* (255 Columbus Avenue) serves good drinks to nostalgic hippies. The *Washington Square Bar and Grill* is some-

what more elegant and has four first-class bartenders; yuppies can be spotted dining in the stylish atmosphere of the *Cypress Club* (500 Jackson Street/corner Montgomery) and in the more rustic setting of the *San Francisco Brewing Company* (155 Columbus Avenue) people sup freshly-brewed dark beer.

But all this is just to whet the appetite. The real "scene" meets in the clubs south of Market Street. SoMa (SOuth of MArket) is the name given to the part of town where warehouses formerly stood, which has become in the course of the last few years the centre of San Francisco night-life. The *DNA Lounge* (375 Eleventh Street) is a two-storeyed disco with walls decorated with pop art. From the gallery there is an excellent view of the dance-floor below.

The latest trend is the "Smart Drink Bar", at which non-alcoholic vitamin drinks are served to restore the energy lost while dancing. *Julie's Supper Club* (1123 Folsom Street/corner Seventh Street) is in the heart of SoMa, a restaurant and bar in the style of the 1950's, which features old-time rock'n'roll in keeping with the atmosphere. *Club DV8* (540 Howard Street/corner First Street) is a modern rock disco in the New York style, housed in a huge warehouse. A little further on (at 177 Town-

send Street) is *Toon Town*, a psychedelic palace with a rather sleazy clientele, laser shows and holographs.

The *OZ*, situated outside the SoMa district, offers entertainment at a higher level, in the truest sense of the word, for this super-chic disco is situated on the top floor of the St. Francis Hotel on Union Square.

If, however, you don't feel like dancing, then it is a good idea to go on a pub crawl through the bars on Union Street or in North Beach, to listen to music and observe people: *Stars* (150 Redwood Alley/Golden Gate Avenue) is one of the most famous bars in San Francisco with a best-dressed clientele; the restaurant adjacent prides itself on its California cuisine.

Good jazz is played in *Harry's* (2020 Fillmore Street) or in *Miss Pearl's Jam House* (601 Eddy Street). And to round off the evening it is worthwhile having a final night-cap in the penthouse bar of one of the large hotels, perhaps in the *View Lounge* of the Marriot (777 Market Street, open until 2.00 am) or to soft, sophisticated jazz in *Club 36* (Grand Hyatt Hotel, on Union Square).

SHOPPING

Nobody needs to go home without souvenirs, for a tourist city like San Francisco has something to meet every taste. The best places for souvenirs are the shops on Fisherman's Wharf, for example in *Ghirardelli Square* (900 North Point). Here you will also find tasteful and useful souvenirs, such as colourful kites.

But there are other things to be considered: sportswear and jeans are reasonably priced in the United States, and the boutiques of San Francisco are famous for their elegant, interesting fashions. The shops and department stores (example Neiman-Marcus) around Union Square and in the *San Francisco Shopping Centre* on Market Street are good places to shop. Designer fashions are to be found in Union Street in the Marina District; American art in the galleries on Sutter Street north of Union Square and for *antique lovers* there are several excellently stocked shops around Jackson Square.

And one tip for something special, if a little heavy, to take home: California wine. You can buy it from the *Napa Vallery Winery Exchange* (415 Taylor Street), for example, or you can, of course, always buy it directly in the Napa valley.

The Union Street Spring Festival on the first weekend in June features entertainers of all sorts.

PHOTOGRAPHY TIPS

Many of the most important sights can be seen by following *Scenic Drive*: In the centre of town, however, you will be well advised to walk or use the cable car to see the Market, Downtown, Nob Hill, the piers, the Civic Centre and Mission District. Chinatown provides the most interesting motifs early in the morning when vegetable and fish are being delivered and in the evening. But make sure you always ask permission before taking photographs!

A good panoramic view can be had from Telegraph Hill (Coit Tower) and Twin Peaks (requires a steady tripod and telephoto lens as it is often very windy, but particularly attractive in the evening). From Hyde/Lombard Street there is a good view of Alcatraz, from the cable car or to the east across the steep bends of Lombard Street. One of the most attractive views of San Francisco is to be had from Alamo Square, of the Victorian houses on *Postcard Row* and the skyscrapers of the downtown skyline (best when light is fading, with a tripod and telephoto lens).

To capture the Golden Gate Bridge, town side: with Fort Point from the Promenade or from the western side in the Presidio; north side: from the parking area east of Route 101 or from the Marin Headlands with the town's skyline in the background. In the morning there is often fog.

From Treasure Island (reached by car across Bay Bridge) there is a magnificent view of downtown San Francisco (Ferry Building) particularly in the evening. In all instances, however, it is much better to avoid the well-known views once the first enthusiasm has waned and set out in search of one's own motifs.

FESTIVALS AND HOLIDAYS

There's a hardly a weekend between Easter and October on which San Francisco does not have something or other to celebrate, either important official celebrations like 4 July or smaller local celebrations in the various parts of the city, where the many immigrant communities keep up the traditions of their homelands.

During the summer months, the city's professional sports teams draw thousands of spectators to their games.

JANUARY. This is the quietest month in the year. The main event is the *New Year's Day Swim*, when a few die-hards jump into the cold waters of the bay (12 degrees Celsius / 54 degrees Fahrenheit) and swim from Alcatraz to the Aquatic Park.

FEBRUARY. *Chinese New Year* usually falls at the beginning of the month and is celebrated for an entire week by the largest Chinese community outside of Asia. The programme includes the Miss Chinatown competition and a colourful parade of dragons down Market, Stockton and Kearny Streets to Columbus Avenue.

MARCH. On *St Patrick's Day*, 17 March, the Irish set out to prove to their patron saint, Patrick, just what hardened drinkers they are, and green beer gushes out of the taps in the Irish pubs along Geary Boulevard. The climax of the celebrations is the parade on Market Street, always on the Sunday nearest to 17 March.

APRIL. At the beginning of the month, the Japanese cherry trees start to flower in Golden Gate Park, an event which San Francisco's Japanese community celebrates with tea ceremonies and a parade from City Hall to Japan Town.
The last Sunday in the month marks the official start of the sailing season in the bay with thousands of boats on a course between Tiburon, Sausalito and the Golden Gate Bridge.

MAY. On 5 May the Latin American community celebrates Mexican Independence Day, *Cinco de Mayo*, with fiestas and parades in the Mission District. On the third Sunday in May more than 100,000

The atmosphere of a fair prevails here all the time. On Pier 39, a little to the east of Fisherman's Wharf.

Spring in San Francisco: white sails hover over the bay, the sky is bright blue and people sit in street cafés wearing light summer clothing. A perfect setting. But then along comes summer, bringing with it the fog which turns lightly-clad tourists into miserable, shivering beings who derive little pleasure from their tour of the city. It makes a good photograph when the fog makes the Golden Gate appear to be packed in cotton-wool, but it has also resulted in many a head cold.

The Bay Area actually has a Mediterranean climate, implying a sunny, dry summer and a somewhat cooler, damp winter. This is certainly true of Oakland and Berkeley and for the other cities on the bay, but not for fog-ridden San Francisco. Here the warmest, sunniest days of the year are in spring and autumn. July and August are dominated by a dramatic in-

FOG: SAN FRANCISCO'S AIR-CONDITIONING

terplay of fog and sun, which can make the temperatures suddenly drop.

Meteorologists, of course, have an explanation for this phenomenon: currents off the coast of northern California draw cold water from the depths of the ocean to the surface. The critical moment comes when the land heats up under the strong California sun and fog forms as a result of the great difference in temperature over the land and the sea.

The white, swirling banks of fog do not stretch far inland as the mountains along the coast block the way, with one exception: the Golden Gate. Here there is nothing to stop the fog from moving into the

bay and enveloping the bridge, Alcatraz and Fisherman's Wharf in damp clouds, Only a few hundred metres further on, the fog disperses as soon as it hits the dry, hot air off the land.

This interplay of the elements keeps the sky continuously in motion and provides the city with a natural system of air-conditioning. Whereas the people living on the broad, windless plain of Los Angeles have to suffer under a thick pall of smog for more than two hundred days of the year, the air in San Francisco is clear with the exception of some twenty days annually. And it is a generally accepted opinion that the antics of the weather at the Golden Gate, the continuous struggle for supremacy between the fog and the sun, makes summer a particularly attractive time to visit San Francisco.

Karl Teuschl

runners participate in the *Bay to Breakers Race*, not a real marathon but a people's run covering twelve kilometres (almost eight miles) from the Embarcadero to the Pacific Ocean. This can be great fun as many of those taking part dress in costume.

JUNE. The first weekend in the month is the date of the *Union Street Spring Festival* with its vendors and street performers. A week later it is the *Haight-Ashbury Street Fair*, held in what was once the hippie district. That same weekend, the best

jugglers, mimes and buskers meet for the *International Street Performers Festival* on Pier 39.

On the last Sunday in June, the *Lesbian and Gay Freedom Day Parade* is held in Market Street; formerly staged as a political demonstration, it has become an opportunity for the city's homosexual community to draw attention to its situation and to the plight of AIDS victims.

JULY. The climax of the *Independence Day* celebrations is the huge firework display on Crissy Field (Presidio) beginning around 9.00 pm on 4 July. On the first weekend in July, the *Jazz and All That Art music festival* is held along Fillmore Street.

AUGUST. There are no major events in this month, but there are a few cultural events which are free of charge: for example, the San Francisco Mime Troupe appears in Golden Gate Park where open-air Shakespeare is also performed.

In addition to this, the professional football season begins for the San Francisco 49ers in Candlestick Park, to the south of the city centre.

Americas on 24th Street in the Mission District. Music is the most important aspect of the *San Francisco Blues Festival*, held in the middle of the month in Fort Mason Centre, when many of the great blues artists of the west coast perform.

On the last weekend in the month or the first in October, the streets of the Castro District are turned into one huge stage when the city's gays turn out to celebrate the *Castro Street Fair*, dancing through the streets in a carefree mood, in costume.

OCTOBER. During the *Columbus Day Celebrations* at the beginning of the month, the Italians of North Beach remember "their" countryman Christopher Columbus and re-enact his landing in the New World in Aquatic Park. This is followed by a blessing of the fishing fleet and a parade from Market Street to Columbus Avenue. The last week in October is de-

and go from house to house, the city's adults celebrate at the *Exotic Erotic Ball* in the Concourse Exhibition Centre.

NOVEMBER. At the end of the month candles are lit on the twenty metre (sixty-six foot) tree in the *Tree Lighting Ceremony* on Pier 39. Let the Christmas season and shopping rush begin!

DECEMBER. On New Year's Eve people gather in Union Square and in North Beach to greet the New Year with a champagne toast.

OFFICIAL HOLIDAYS:
New Year's Day: 1 January
Martin Luther King Day: 15 January
President's Birthday: third Monday in February
Memorial Day: last Monday in May, beginning of summer

A view to the northeast from Twin Peaks. In the foreground are typical gabled houses, in the distance the harbour and east shore of the bay.

SEPTEMBER. On the first weekend in the month Sausalito holds its *Art Festival*, with celebrations in the streets and many exhibitions of artists' works. A week later the Latinos exhibit their folk art and demonstrate their cuisine at the *Festival de las*

voted to jazz: ten large concerts attract musicians from all over the world to take part in the *Jazz in the City Festival*. And finally there is *Hallowe'en* on 31 October, one of the most important carnivals for Americans. While the children dress up

Fourth of July: Independence Day
Labor Day: first Monday in September
Columbus Day: second Monday in Oct.
Veterans' Day: 11 November
Thanksgiving: fourth Thursday in Nov.
Christmas Day: 25 December

OVERVIEW

Anyone who wants to get a general, overall impression of the various sights is advised to drive the seventy-nine kilometres (forty-nine miles) of the clearly posted *Scenic Drive* (information from the Visitors' Information Centre). It is advisable to allow a whole day for the drive.

POINTS OF INTEREST

Circled numbers refer to the map on page 48, those in italics refer to the colour photographs.

ALCATRAZ ①. The famous "prison rock", barely five hundred metres (1,640 feet) long, which was originally given its name by the Spaniards because of the pelicans (*alcatraces*) that nested there, was first used by the army as a disciplinary camp in the nineteenth century. It acquired its rather bleak reputation as a federal high security prison much later, between 1933 and 1963. Al Capone was imprisoned here for five years, as was Robert Stroud, the bird-man of Alcatraz, who became a world-famous ornithologist while imprisoned here. Breaking out of Alcatraz was

Daring design: St. Mary's Cathedral.

considered to be an impossibility and indeed only five inmates ever succeeded and they were never heard of again. It is assumed that they drowned in the icy waters of the bay and in the dangerous currents around the island. After the prison was closed, Red Indian activists occupied the island for nineteen months in 1969. It has been open to the public since 1973 and can be reached with the Red and White fleet boats from Pier 41. *21, 47*

CASTRO DISTRICT ②. Castro Street in the *Mission District*, roughly between 17th Street and 19th Street, has been the home of San Francisco's homosexual commun-

ity since the 1960's. There are trendy restaurants, bars and shops selling leather goods along the streets. A sight well worth a visit is the *Castro Theatre* ② (429 Castro Street/Market Street), a nostalgic cinema in the Moorish style dating from 1922.

Grant Street, a typical scene in Chinatown.

CHINATOWN. Eight streets on either side of Grant Avenue, approximately between Bush Street and Broadway. This is Chinatown, the largest Chinese settlement outside of Asia with almost 80,000 residents. The district was founded during the years of the gold rush, around 1850, as a home for the first Chinese immigrants who came to California as cheap labourers. For many years these immigrants from China were considered by the Americans to be the "yellow peril". After World War II they were allowed to buy land only in the district now known as Chinatown so that an isolated community gradually developed, a town within a town.

Even though many Chinese people, and particularly the wealthier ones, live in other parts of San Francisco today, Chinatown has retained its exotic atmosphere and is still the economic and cultural centre of the Chinese community in the city. Along the main street, Grant Avenue, souvenir stores and import/export shops offer jade jewellery, bamboo baskets and the typical tableware inset with grains of rice. But the side-streets and Stockton Street are where Chinese everyday life flourishes: there are butchers' shops, laundries, shops selling herbs and small restaurants all jostling for position in these busy streets.

The main architectural features of interest are the *Dragon Gate* ④ on Grant Avenue, the *Bank of Canton* ⑤ (743 Washington Street) built in 1909 in the style of a pagoda, the *Tin How Temple* ⑥ (125 Waverly Place) and the façades of the old hostels of the *Family Benevolent Associations* around Waverly Place and Washington

Street. These family organizations offer help to anyone of the same name: No 39, for example, is the house belonging to the Wang Association. *9, 10, 17, 24/25, 26, 27*

CIVIC CENTRE ⑦. San Francisco's administrative centre, which was completely rebuilt after the earthquake in 1906, lies slightly north of Market Street on the western edge of the downtown. The buildings around Civic Centre Plaza are dominated by *City Hall* ⑧, a rather bombastic building. The dome is 92 metres (302 feet) high, taller than that of the Capitol in Washington. The other buildings around the Plaza and in the same Classical style as the City Hall are the *Main Public Library* ⑨ and the *Civic Auditorium* ⑩. The most

City Hall is modelled on St Peter's in Rome.

interesting buildings, however, are those situated behind City Hall: the *War Memorial Opera House* ⑪, built in 1932, was where the inaugural meeting of the United Nations took place in 1945; the *Louise M. Davies Symphony Hall*, opened in 1980, is the home of the San Francisco Symphony Orchestra.

There is nothing surprising in the fact that homeless people are often seen in the area around City Hall, for on the one hand demonstrations are usually staged at the centre of authority and on the other *Tenderloin District*, one of the poorest, most dangerous areas of town, starts just to the north of the Civic Centre.

The Main Public Library dates from 1917.

The skyscrapers of the Financial District.

CLIFF HOUSE. See entry under "Golden Gate National Recreation Area".

EMBARCADERO CENTRE ⑫. This complex of skyscrapers, which was erected on the eastern edge of the Financial District between 1967 and 1981, is considered to be a very successful example of modern architecture and town planning. This "city in the city" covers more than four hectares (ten acres). The heart of the complex consists of five narrow office blocks which are linked together by pedestrian bridges. There are elegant shops, restaurants and cafés on the three lower levels, at their busiest at midday. There are plenty of seats to tempt shoppers to rest for awhile. In summer, open-air concerts are held on *Justin Herman Plaza* ⑬, on the eastern side of the centre, with the *Vaillancourt Fountain* as a setting; the fountain is referred to by the San Franciscans in a show of wry humour as "ten on the Richter scale", and the chaotic structure of cement pipes does indeed look as if it has been involved in an earthquake.

The lobby of the *Hyatt Regency Hotel* ⑭, built in 1973 between the Embarcadero Centre and Market Street, is of particular interest: in the inner courtyard of the twenty-storey building is Charles Perry's monumental sculpture "Eclipse". *15*

FINANCIAL DISTRICT. The banking district to the north of Market Street, the "Wall Street of the West Coast", is San Francisco's heart. With its reflecting glass and concrete towers it dominates the city skyline, even though these palaces of high finance are not actually standing on the firmest of foundations; the whole site east of Montgomery Street was filled in to make space for construction, beneath it is the former prospectors' harbour including hundreds of deserted ships. The centre of the financial district is roughly the point at which Montgomery Street crosses California Street, the site of the city's highest building, the fifty-two-storey *Bank of America* ⑮ with a very good restaurant on the top floor.

The most famous building in the financial district, the *Transamerica Pyramid* ⑯, has only four storeys less and lies further north on Montgomery Street. But while all these buildings are ultra-modern skyscrapers, there are still some buildings in the district dating from the 1920's and 1930's, including the *Pacific Stock Exchange* (Pine Street/Sansome Street) and the *Merchant's Exchange Building* from 1903 (405 California Street). The shopping centres in the district are also extremely modern, for example the *Crocker Galleria* on Post Street. *6/7, 10, 14, 31*

FISHERMAN'S WHARF ⑰ is a favourite place for a stroll and the heart of the city's tourist trade. No visitor to San Francisco should miss going to this busy part of town with its shops and restaurants. The old, romantic atmosphere of the former fishing harbour of the Italian immigrants has long gone. Today mass tourism is the order of the day. A small bucket of shrimp from one of the market-sellers is still an intrinsic part of the visit, just as is a shopping expedition in search of souvenirs through *The Cannery* ⑱, formerly a fish factory, and *Ghirardelli Square* ⑲, formerly a chocolate factory, past boutiques, curiosity shops and artists selling jewellery.

The latest addition to the district is *Pier 39* ⑳. This reconstructed harbour pier has become a favourite spot with street artists. *12, 28, 29*

FORT MASON CENTRE ㉑. The huge barracks and docks of the old military base west of the *Aquatic Park* were used as soldiers' quarters prior to deployments to the Pacific theatre of operation during World War II. The army handed over the site to

Entertainment under a blue sky: Pier 39

the city in 1972. The barracks were renovated and a cultural centre with several small museums, artists' workshops, galleries and theatres came into being. The vegetarian restaurant *Greens* in the Zen Centre is to be recommended. The five kilometres (three miles) of the *Golden Gate Promenade* ㉒ stretch from the western entrance of Fort Mason to the Golden Gate Bridge. *35*

GOLDEN GATE BRIDGE ㉓. This is the symbol of San Francisco and perhaps the most beautiful suspension bridge in the world, the ideal place for would-be suicides and a nightmare for the men who have to paint it. The bridge over the narrows at the Golden Gate has been having its own particular effect on people for more than fifty years. Here are a few statistics: the six-lane road over the bridge is some seventy metres (230 feet) above sea-level, the two red pylons tower 227 metres (745 feet). The bridge is 2.8 kilometres (1.7 miles) long.

Construction lasted from 1933 to 1937, at a cost of thirty-five million dollars. It is used by almost fifty million vehicles in the course of a year. The man who built it, Joseph B. Strauss, would never have dreamed of such figures; he planned the bridge originally for three to four million cars a year.

Two vantage points, at the ends of the northern and southern approach roads to the bridge, offer magnificent views of both the bridge and the city. The best time to walk across the bridge is late afternoon when the sun bathes the skyline of San Francisco in a charming light. *2, 34, 46*

The Cannery, an entertainment centre.

GOLDEN GATE NATIONAL RECREATION AREA ㉔. This is a national park maintained by the federal government and includes many historical buildings around the Golden Gate, as well as beaches, parks and other recreation areas

EARTHQUAKES

California is not only the mecca of film and television producers, it is also the region of the United States most frequently hit by earthquakes. California's coastline is more than 1,600 kilometres (one thousand miles) long and borders the Pacific basin, from which eighty percent of all the earth's earthquakes originate. In California itself, there are hundreds of faults, which result in more than a thousand quakes every year, more than half of which are only felt by animals or seismographs. The worst of the earthquakes usually originate in the San Andreas fault, which is hundreds of kilometres in length and runs more or less parallel with the California coastline. San Francisco lies only a few kilometres north of the fault.

It was clear from the days of Mark Twain that San Francisco could suffer a quake.

It wasn't earth tremors but fire which destroyed most building in the earthquake of 1906.

But that "Bagdad on the Bay" could be reduced to debris and ashes in a matter of seconds, an area of ten square kilometres (four square miles), was unbelievable. Terror struck the sleeping town between 5.12 and 5.13 am on the morning of 18 April 1906. San Francisco was very near to the epicentre of an earthquake which shook some 129,500 square kilometres (50,000 square miles) of California for fifty-five seconds; it was the most severe earthquake in the state's history. The major tremors registered 8.3 on the open-ended Richter scale.

One of the first buildings to collapse was City Hall, which had cost seven million dollars to build. Still half asleep, the residents of San Francisco stumbled out into the trembling streets. Enrico Caruso, who was appearing in the city at the time, wrapped a towel round his neck to protect his vocal cords and rushed down Market Street clutching an original photograph of President Roosevelt in his hand. But there was nothing anecdotal about the bricks and tiles that came raining down, the bursts in the gas and water pipes, and when, in addition, the sewers burst open, the smell of burning, mingled with the fumes from the sewers to produce an acid stench.

Twenty-four hours of chaos followed. Thousands of people slept in the parks while fire destroyed what the earthquake had spared. Thirty-eight horse-drawn fire engines fought a hopeless battle against fifty-two huge fires in the course of the next three days. By the time the fire had been brought under control, by blowing up the villas along Van Ness Avenue, 452 people were dead and more than eighty percent of the town's buildings had been destroyed. Hundreds of people were missing and three hundred thousand had been made homeless (three quarters of San Francisco's population in those days). Twenty thousand buildings had been destroyed, the damage totalling between four and five hundred million dollars.

The earthquake made the people of San Francisco all the more determined not to give in to the whims of nature. The city was rebuilt on the same site in a demonstration of unbroken optimism. However new measures were taken to ensure a greater degree of security in the case of further quakes. Twenty thousand new buldings were erected within the next three years and at the end of five years, a newly-born San Francisco shone gaily over the bay.

The measures undertaken to make the buildings quake-proof proved their worth when on 17 October 1989 a severe earthquake measuring 7.1 on the Richter scale hit San Francisco. The damage was not too excessive; the electricity supply was cut and the population anxious, but something else had happened which nobody had reckoned with: the Bay Bridge was badly damaged and part of the upper lane collapsed on to the lower lane of the Nimitz Freeway.

Earthquakes are simply a part of everyday life in California. Nobody makes a fuss about them. Since 1989, however, many a motorist has driven the long way round to avoid the freeways, and people are more aware of the dangers of another earthquake. Which is why you will find in the San Francisco telephone directory not only all the subscribers' numbers but also the most important points to bear in mind in the case of an earthquake.

Wolfgang J. Fuchs

At the entrance to the Japanese Tea Garden.

in San Francisco. The island of *Alcatraz* ① and *Angel Island*, once a quarantine station for Asian immigrants, are also part of the recreation area, as is the *National Maritime Museum* ㉕, *Fort Mason*, the area of the *Presidio* and the old fortifications of *Fort Point* ㉖ at the foot of the Golden Gate Bridge. North of the bridge almost all of the *Marin Headlands* are part of the recreation area, those bare, windy hills along the Pacific coast where the bustle of the city seems miles away.
Cliff House, on the westernmost tip of San Francisco, is also part of the Golden Gate National Recreation Area. This famous restaurant, with its magnificent view of the Pacific Ocean and the seal rocks off the coast, has already been rebuilt five times after fires. *21, 35, 47*

GOLDEN GATE PARK ㉗. The city of San Francisco bought, in the 1870's, the 800 metre (2,625 feet) wide piece of land which stretches from the Pacific some five kilometres (three miles) into the city centre in order to lay out a park. But it was many years before the bare dunes took on their present appearance of formal gardens with small clusters of eucalyptus trees, picnic areas and sports fields. John McLaren, a Scotsman, was in charge of

Enjoying a lunch break in Golden Gate Park.

work on the park for fifty-six years beginning in 1887. He had exotic trees and shrubs planted, paths and lakes created, gradually making the park the most popular recreation area in town.
Most of the tourist attractions are to be found in the eastern part of the park, around the *Music Concourse* ㉘; museums such as the *California Academy of Sciences*, the *M. H. de Young Memorial Museum* and the *Japanese Tea Garden*, laid out in 1894, which attracts many visitors with its cherry blossoms.
A little further east in the park is the *Conservatory of Flowers*, a greenhouse constructed in the style of those in London's Kew Gardens. To the south of the Music Concourse is the *Strybing Arboretum and Botanical Gardens*.
The western part of the park, which stretches to the coast, has paths for strolling, a buffalo enclosure and a golf course. It is peaceful in comparison to the eastern region. Golden Gate Park is busiest on Sundays when the open spaces and paths become a stage for roller-skaters and other people who enjoy displaying their talents. *38, 39, 40/41*

MARINA DISTRICT/PACIFIC HEIGHTS.
These two districts in the northern part of San Francisco are amongst the most attractive and expensive residential areas in town. Magnificent old villas with Victorian façades and beautifully-tended gardens line the streets around Alta Plaza Park; the architecture is picturesque, with towers and ornamentation. The *Marina District* is the younger of the two and not quite as

exclusive. It was built on the rubble from the earthquake of 1906, which was simply thrown into the bay. The district was the hardest hit by the earthquake in 1989. The most striking building in the Marina District is the *Palace of Fine Arts* ㉙, a domed building with pillars and statues which was originally built to house the Panama Pacific World Exhibition in 1915. It now houses the Exploratorium. The main street in the district is *Union Street* ㉚, which is pleasant for window-shopping. *37*

MARKET STREET ㉛. San Francisco's main thoroughfare runs diagonally across the otherwise rectangular plan of downtown streets. It was planned in 1847 to be a magnificent boulevard, forty metres (131 feet) wide, and now serves as a dividing line between the business district to the north of the harbour and the warehouse district to the south. Its most important contribution today is to local public transport: buses and tram-cars roll along it and the trains of the BART underground railway system run below it.
Market Street starts in the east at the bay, in front of the *Ferry Building* ㉜, the tower of

Before the Golden Gate Bridge was built the Ferry Building was the symbol of San Francisco.

which, dating from 1896, survived the earthquake in 1906. Before the main bridges were built in the 1930's, this ferry terminal was San Francisco's link with the north. Moving west from this point, Market Street first cuts through the *Financial District* and then the busy city centre; the most important things to see are the small *Chevron Oil Museum* in the *Standard Oil Building* (557 Market Street) as well as the interior of the somewhat overpowering *Sheraton Palace Hotel* ③③ (2 New Montgomery Street).

The cable cars start their journey over the hills to the north and Fisherman's Wharf from Hallidie Plaza. Across the road, at the corner of Fifth Street, stands the city's latest shopping centre, the *San Francisco Centre* ③④.

Moving further west, Market Street passes the *Civic Centre* and then ends in the *Castro District*, the home of San Francisco's gay community. *6/7, 10, 34*

MISSION DISTRICT. This part of the city owes its name to the Mission of San Francisco de Asis, commonly known as *Mission Dolores* ③⑤. Franciscan monks established the sixth mission on California's soil here in 1776, a mission out of which the town of San Francisco was to develop. The small adobe church, the town's oldest building, has survived every earthquake. There is a small museum documenting the history of the mission.

More than five thousand Red Indians lie buried in the mission's graveyard, victims of the two measles epidemics in the early nineteenth century.

The Mission District, with its main street, *Mission Street*, was traditionally San Francisco's immigrant district, the springboard for newcomers into a better life. In former times, Germans, Irish and Italians all lived here; today it is the Mexicans, Nicaraguans and Philippinos who demonstrate their cultural traditions in the many parades, fiestas and community festivities. *36*

NOB HILL. This hill, approximately one hundred metres (three hundred-thirty feet) above sea-level, lies due west of Chinatown. It was the most fashionable residential area of San Francisco towards the end of the last century. Extremely wealthy Nabobs (the name Nob resulted from a shortening of this term), among them three of the most famous railway magnates – Mark Hopkins, Leland Stafford and Charles Crocker – built breath-taking establishments for themselves on the hill. Most of this magnificence fell victim to the fires after the earthquake of 1906, though Nob Hill remains the best address in San Francisco. Some of the city's most beautiful hotels, for example the *Fairmont* and the *Mark Hopkins*, both of which have panorama restaurants on the top floor, are also in this district. *Grace Cathedral* ③⑥, a church built in the style of Paris' Notre Dame, is also worth seeing.

Nob Hill was made famous by many films, such as Hitchcock's "Vertigo". The steep streets of the district have also been used in many chase scenes, and will, therefore, seem somewhat familiar. *18/19*

NORTH BEACH. This is where the exotic smells from nearby *Chinatown* mingle with the aroma of freshly-roasted coffee beans and steaming pizzas from the Italian trattorias. This is where the sonorous sounds from the blues bars melt with the superficial rattling of piano keys from the strip clubs to create the pulsating melody of the city. North Beach, the former Italian quarter around Washington Square, is today one of the liveliest districts of San Francisco.

The district became famous during the 1950's when the poets of the beat generation lived here: Allen Ginsberg, Jack Kerouac and Lawrence Ferlinghetti. The *City Lights Bookstore* ③⑦ (261 Columbus Avenue), founded in those days to be a meeting-place for men of letters, is still here, as are several established cosy cafés and excellent Italian restaurants. *37*

will most interest visitors: it runs along the cliffs with a marvellous view of Golden Gate Bridge. Visitors are also advised to visit *Fort Point* ②⑦, completed in 1861, at the foot of the bridge. It was erected originally as a fortification and used to house building materials and workers during the four years it took to finish the bridge.

SAN FRANCISCO-OAKLAND BAY BRIDGE ③⑨. This, San Francisco's second largest bridge, is by no means as famous as the Golden Gate Bridge, but it is just as much a wonder of technology. Thirteen kilometres (eight miles) long, it links the city via Treasure Island with the port of Oakland in the East Bay. It was the longest bridge in the world when it was opened in 1936. *35*

SOMA. The part of San Francisco known as *South of Market* was a district neglected for many years, an area around the harbour with warehouses falling into disrepair, sleazy pubs and disreputable stores. But all this has changed in the last ten years. The city put up a new congress centre on the corner of Howard and Third Street, the *Mascone Convention Centre*,

There is a magnificent view of Russion Hill from the park in Washington Square.

PRESIDIO ③⑧. The northernmost point of the San Francisco peninsula has been a military area ever since the time of the Spanish rule. The six hundred hectares (1,483 acres) of the hilly site are today the headquarters of the US Sixth Army, with homes for the soldiers and a large military cemetery. It is Lincoln Boulevard which

named after Mayor Mascone who was murdered in 1978, and gradually began to polish up the district.

Many artists moved into the warehouses, owing to the low rents, and were followed by galleries, restaurants and other trendy places. A small colony of houseboats has established itself in *China Basin* ④⓪.

TELEGRAPH HILL ㊸. There is an excellent view to be had from Telegraph Hill and it can be easily gained on foot, either from the west via Filbert Street from Washington Square or by climbing the Filbert Steps which, flanked by greenery, stretch from the Embarcadero some hundred metres up the hill. As a reward for the strenuous climb there is a breathtaking view of the bay, the Golden Gate, Fisherman's Wharf and Alcatraz. *Coit Tower*, presented to the town by Lillien H. Coit, the banker's widow, stands on the top of the hill and has a lift to make the last stage of the ascent easier. *22, 29*

TWIN PEAKS ㊶. This double hill stands 275 metres (902 feet) above sea-level in the southwestern part of San Francisco and is considered to offer one of the best views of the city. Market Street runs straight to the bay from the foot of the hill with the towering skyline of the financial district in the foreground. The best time to visit Twin Peaks is late in the afternoon when the setting sun bathes the skyscrapers in a golden light, or in the evening when there is a carpet of lights flickering all around. *6/7, 32/33*

stands the venerable old *St. Francis Hotel* dating from 1904. *Maiden Lane*, a narrow lane leading off the square to the east, used to be the red light district but is today an attractive pedestrian precinct with galleries and elegant boutiques. *11*

MUSEUMS

ANSEL ADAMS CENTER/FRIENDS OF PHOTOGRAPHY. One of the five rooms of this museum of photography is devoted to the works of the great landscape photographer Ansel Adams. The others are used to mount changing exhibitions of the works of young artists.
250 Fourth Street, Tuesday to Sunday, 11.00 am to 6.00 pm.

ASIAN ART MUSEUM. One of the best collections of art from the Far East in the world was donated by the former president of the International Olympic Committee, Avery Brundage.
Golden Gate Park, Wednesday to Sunday, 10.00 am to 5.00 pm.

CABLE CAR MUSEUM. See insert text on page 20.

CALIFORNIA PALACE OF THE LEGION OF HONOUR. In this magnificent building from 1924, a copy of the Palais de la Légion d'Honneur in Paris, the works only of French masters from the Middle Ages to the twentieth century are on display. A comprehensive collection of the works of Rodin is an important part of the exhibition.
Lincoln Park, Wednesday to Sunday, 10.00 am to 5.00 pm.

CHINESE HISTORICAL SOCIETY OF AMERICA. Photographs and documents concerning the history of the Chinese in the American west are featured.
650 Commercial Street, Tuesday to Saturday, 12 noon to 4.00 pm.

EXPLORATORIUM. The setting of this museum alone is impressive: the bombastic Palace of Fine Arts, a hall remaining from the Panama Pacific Exhibition of 1915. Inside there is science to touch. A spectacular part of this museum of science and technology is the Tactile Gallery, a labyrinth without any light.
3601 Lyon Street, Tuesday to Sunday, 10.00 am to 5.00 pm, Wednesday to 9.30 pm.

A favourite spot with football and baseball players and morning joggers: Marina Park along the coast near Fort Mason.

UNION SQUARE ㊷. This small square with its palm trees, below which there is a huge underground garage, is the centre of the shopping and business district north of Market Street. Famous department stores such as Macy's, travel agencies, jewellers' and many other shops line the streets. On the western side of the square

CALIFORNIA ACADEMY OF SCIENCE. This is a large science museum consisting of exhibition galleries, an aquarium, planetarium and laserium. There are also good exhibitions devoted to the natural history of California.
Golden Gate Park, daily 10.00 am to 5.00 pm, in summer until 7.00 pm.

FORT MASON CENTRE. This site in the Marina District dates from World War II and today houses the *Mexican Museum*, the *Museo Italo-Americano*, the *Craft and Folk Art Museum* as well as the SS Jeremiah O'Brien. The museums are usually closed Monday and Tuesday, the ship is only open to visitors at the weekend.

Two kilometres (just over one mile) off the coast of San Francisco in the bay lies the island of Alcatraz, a clearly visible indication of an unbroken struggle against crime and one of the most secure federal prisons in the years from 1933 to 1963. In those thirty years there were never more than two hundred-fifty prisoners on the island at one time, and as a result of the long sentences which were served here, there were, in fact, scarcely more than fifteen hundred men ever imprisoned "on the rock". The most infamous inmates were Al Capone, the gangster; Alvin Karpis, the bank robber-kidnapper; George "Machine Gun" Kelly; and "Doc Barker". One prisoner actually became famous during his stay: Robert Stroud, the Bird Man of Alcatraz, became a reputable ornithologist while in prison. When the prison was closed down, Red Indians tried to take over the unused island both in 1964 and in 1969, in order to draw attention to their land rights on and around the bay. Their efforts were, however, in vain, and after two severe winters, most of them had willingly left the inhos-

WHERE AL CAPONE RETIRED ...

dians, during World War I conscientious objectors, political reactionaries and union agitators have all been imprisoned on Alcatraz at some time.

Finally, in 1933, Alcatraz was turned into a high security prison against the background of rising crime during the Depression and the prohibition years. James A. Johnson was the first of four governors on Alcatraz. He equipped the prison in such a ways as to make escape virtually impossible. And indeed, only George Raft, E. G. Robinson, Clint Eastwood and John Paul Scott ever managed to escape, the first three on film.

Only Scott escaped in real life, swimming across the bay to the shore. His escape exhausted him so, that he was easily recaptured on the beach. There were twenty-six attempted escapes in all; eight escapees were either shot or drowned, thirteen were recaptured, five are still missing. It is assumed that they also drowned.

Top: Al Capone in 1930. Bottom left: A prison riot caused a sensation in 1946. Bottom right: "The rock" in 1964, a year after the prison was closed.

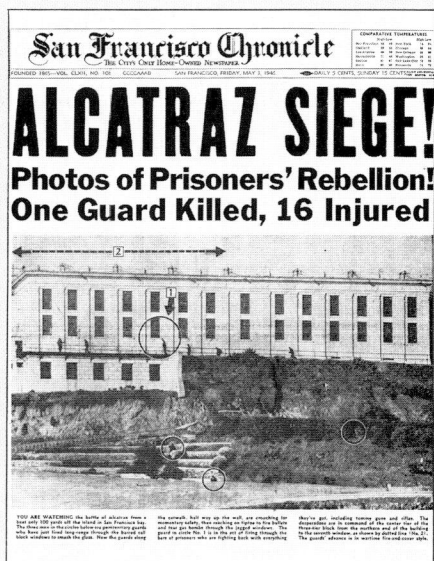

pitable island by the time the last fifteen were deported. Alcatraz has been open to the public since 1973.

The island owes its name to the Spanish explorer Juan Manuel de Ayala, who called it Isla de los Alcatraces, island of the pelicans, in 1775. In general, the public only began to take an interest in this bare, rocky island in the years following the California gold rush.

In 1853, the first structure was constructed on the island, a lighthouse. A short time thereafter, a fortress was erected. The American army transformed it for use in the defense of the Bay of San Francisco. When this was no longer necessary, the army used the island as a military prison.

Deserters from the army during the Spanish-American War, rebellious In-

Alcatraz was closed in 1963 as methods in the penal system had changed and "the fortress" was costing the taxpayer fifteen dollars a day, the most expensive of the federal prisons. During the thirty years the prison was in operation, the four hundred-fifty cells were never half full to capacity. At times, the number of guards on duty numbered more than the prisoners.

Wolfgang J. Fuchs

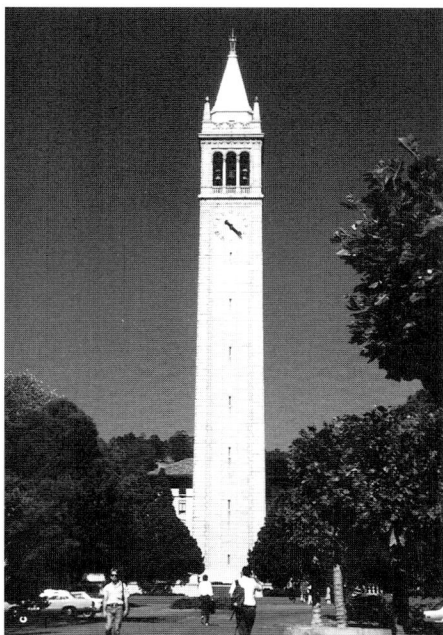

Sather Tower, Berkeley's "campanile".

HAAS-LILIENTHAL HOUSE. Of the fourteen thousand buildings in San Francisco which survived the earthquake of 1906, this house, built by Peter R. Schmidt in 1886 for William Haas from Bavaria, is the only one still to be furnished in the Victorian style. The most striking feature of the so-called Eastlake Style which characterizes the house is the asymetrical use of cylinders, globes, pyramids and cubes as well as the architectural prominence of the Queen Anne Tower.

The San Francisco Museum of Modern Art.

2007 Franklin Street, Wednesday 12 noon to 3.15 pm, Sunday 11.00 am to 4.15 pm.

M.H. DE YOUNG MEMORIAL MUSEUM. The oldest museum in San Francisco is named after the newspaper publisher and patron of the arts Michael H. de Young. It has forty rooms in which most of the exhibits are American paintings, sculptures and furniture as well as African, Asian and European works of art from all periods.

Houseboats and floating homes have become a typical sight in the fishing village of Sausalito.

Golden Gate Park, Wednesday to Sunday, 10.00 am to 5.00 pm.

MUSEUM OF MODERN ART. Devoted mainly to collections of European and American art of the twentieth century, the museum concentrates particularly on contemporary California art.
Civic Center, Van Ness Avenue, Tuesday to Friday, 10.00 am to 5.00 pm; Thursday to 9.00 pm; Saturday and Sunday, 11.00 am to 5.00 pm.

NATIONAL MARITIME MUSEUM. Model ships, maps and photographs all testify to the history of seafaring off the West Coast. The collections of the museum are distributed in different locations. At Pier 43 the "Balclutha", the last ship of the Cape Horn fleet, is at anchor. Among the five ships docked at the Hyde Street Pier is the "Eureka", a ferry which operated between Marin County and Oakland.
Aquatic Park, daily 10.00 am to 5.00 pm.

THE TECH MUSEUM. A short distance outside San Francisco but well worth the journey for computer fans is this collection devoted to the achievements of the Silicone Valley.
145 W. San Carlos Street, San José, Tuesday to Sunday, 10.00 am to 5.00 pm.

WELLS FARGO HISTORY ROOM. The company which made its name during the days of the stage-coach exhibits relics from the days of the gold rush.
420 Montgomery Street, Monday to Friday, 9.00 am to 5.00 pm.

EXCURSIONS

No visit to San Francisco would be complete without one or more excursions into the surrounding Bay Area. Here are a few possibilities:

BERKELEY. At the other end of the Bay Bridge lies the busy port of *Oakland*, with 370,000 residents the third largest city on San Francisco Bay. However, of greater interest than Oakland itself is the student town of Berkeley adjoining it to the north, where the *University of California* has one of its most famous campuses on the hills overlooking the bay.
There are several small museums on the three hundred hectares (741 acres) of the campus, including the Pacific Film Archive and the Palestine Institute with its collection of archeological finds.

MUIR WOODS/SAUSALITO. Some twenty kilometres (twelve miles) north of the Golden Gate Bridge on Highway 1, a side road branches off to the *Muir Woods National Monument*, a grove of redwoods, the tallest trees in the world. There are footpaths along the slopes of Mount Tamalpais, 2,571 metres (8,435 feet), throughout the length of this ancient little forest with its giant trees, eighty metres (262 feet) high.

On the way back it is a good idea to make a stop in *Sausalito*, an old artists' colony and fishing village directly north of the Golden Gate Bridge.

Tourism has long since taken over Sausalito and its famous colony of houseboats, but this has not detracted from the charm of the cafés along the waterfront and the artisans' shops in *Bridgeway*, the main street. This is a picturesque place to sit with a drink and watch the skyline of San Francisco. There are ferries from here to the city.

NAPA VALLEY. This is a sunny valley some twenty-two hectares (fifty-four acres) in size in which Chardonnay, Zinfandel and Riesling vines ripen and thrive to produce wines the quality of which has often beaten many a top European wine in competition.

Spanish padres first planted vines in California in the eighteenth century to make wine for mass, but it was only about a hundred years ago that the first real vintners arrived in the Napa Valley. In more recent years large companies have discovered the commercial attractions of grape-growing: Coca Cola has a winery here as does the Walt Disney Co.; many of the wineries belong to Japanese owners who specialize in making rice wine.

The Napa Valley is a short one hundred kilometres (sixty miles) from San Francisco, first via the Golden Gate Bridge and then following US 101 in a northerly direction, continuing on routes 37 and 29. Highway 29 is in fact the main road through the valley with wineries located along it between *Yountville* and *St. Helena*.

The *Robert Mondavi Winery* in Rutherford has excellent guided tours and keen wine drinkers will find many things of interest in the adjoining vinotheque.

To enjoy a real wine-tasting, however, you should drive on further after the guided tour to a smaller winery: the *Rutherford Hill Winery* (north of Rutherford on the Silverado Trail) has, for example, an excellent Cabernet Sauvignon.

YOSEMITE NATIONAL PARK. This huge national park (3,080 square kilometres/1,189 square miles) in the Sierra Nevada Mountains is almost a day's journey east from San Francisco (some 300 kilometres/180 miles), but it is nonetheless one of California's most exciting beauty sports. Gigantic *sequoias*, some of which are three thousand years old, are to be found here, as is California's beautiful *Yosemite Valley*. The steep rock faces drop some thousand metres (3,280 feet) into the valley of the Merced River.

Spring is the best time of year to visit the park, when the melting snow feeds the waterfalls. But whenever you decide to go, you should make a hotel reservation in advance: Yosemite is California's most popular national park and always fully booked as a consequence.

LIST OF SOURCES

Edgar M. Branch (ed.), *Clemens of the Call. Mark Twain in San Francisco.* Berkeley: University of California Press, 1969

Cora Older, *San Francisco. Magic City.* New York: Longmans, Green & Co., 1961

Martin Ridge; Ray Allen Billington (eds.), *America's Frontier Story. A Documentary History of Westward Expansion.* New York: Holt, Rinehart & Winston, 1969

Mark Twain, *Roughing It.* Volume II. New York: Harper and Brothers, 1899

Merrill Windsor, *America's Sunshine Coast.* Washington: National Geographic Society, 1978

George Young, *San Francisco by Cable Car.* San Francisco: Wingbow Books, 1984

We would like to thank all copyright holders and publishers for their kind permission to reprint. Despite intensive efforts on our part, we were not able to contact all copyright holders. Those to whom this applies are asked to contact us.

LIST OF ILLUSTRATIONS

The map on page 48 was drawn by Astrid Fischer-Leitl, Munich.

Gerhard P. Müller, Dortmund: page 54.

Süddeutscher Verlag, Munich: page 34 middle; page 58 top.

Ullstein Bilderdienst, Berlin: page 58 bottom; page 62 top; page 62 lower right.

DESTINATION SAN FRANCISCO
WINDSOR BOOKS INTERNATIONAL, 1993

© English Text by Verlag C.J. Bucher GmbH, Munich 1993

Translation: Susan Bollinger
Editor: Karen Lemiski
Anthology: Karen Lemiski

Grape growing in the Napa Valley is an important branch of agriculture in California.